KISSING THE POPE

NICK DARKE

Nick Darke was born in Wadebridge, Cornwall, in 1948. He was
an actor for eight years before turning to writing in 1978. His
plays include: *Never say Rabbit in a Boat* (Victoria Theatre, Stoke-
on-Trent, 1978); *Landmarks* (Lyric Studio, Hammersmith, 1979);
Say Your Prayers (Joint Stock, Riverside Studios, Hammersmith,
1980); *The Catch* (Royal Court Theatre Upstairs, 1980); a one-act
play, *High Water* (Warehouse, 1980); *The Body* (RSC, The Pit,
1983); *Farmers' Arms* (BBC-TV Film, 1983); *The Earth Turned
Inside Out* (Community Play, St. Austell, 1985); *The Oven-Glove
Murders* (Bush Theatre, 1986); *The Dead Monkey* (RSC, The Pit,
1986); *Ting Tang Mine* (National Theatre, Cottesloe, 1987). In
1979, he was a recipient of the George Devine Award.

By the same author

The Body
Ting Tang Mine and other plays

NICK DARKE
KISSING THE POPE
A PLAY AND A DIARY FOR NICARAGUA

NICK HERN BOOKS

A division of Walker Books Limited

A Nick Hern Book

Kissing The Pope, a play and a diary first published in 1990 as an original paperback by Nick Hern Books, a division of Walker Books Limited, 87 Vauxhall Walk, London SE11 5HJ

Kissing The Pope, a play and a diary © 1990 by Nick Darke

Front cover illustration reproduced by permission of Jenny Mathews/Network Photographers.

Set in Baskerville by Action Typesetting Ltd, Gloucester and printed and bound in Great Britain by Biddles Ltd, Guildford and King's Lynn

British Library Cataloguing in Publication Data
Darke, Nick, 1948-
    Kissing the Pope: a play and a diary for Nicaragua.
    I. Title
    823'.914

ISBN 1 – 85459 – 047 – 2

Caution
All rights whatsoever in this play are strictly reserved. Requests to reproduce the text in whole or in part should be addressed to the publisher. Application for performance in any medium or for translation into any language should be addressed to the author's sole agent, Margaret Ramsay Ltd, 14a Goodwin's Court, St Martin's Lane, London WC2N 4LL.

For the people of Nicaragua

DIARY

Introduction

Nicaragua is a country of the combined size of
England and Wales. It spans the Central American isthmus with
Costa Rica to the south and Honduras to the north. In spite of
its size, Nicaragua's population numbers a mere three million,
half of whom are under the age of fifteen.

For forty years, up until 19 July 1979, Nicaragua was ruled by
a dynasty of dictators named Somoza. Underwritten by
Washington, its hallmark was terror. Whilst the Somozas grew
immeasurably wealthy, the people of Nicaragua remained
malnourished, illiterate and landless. The Somozas' instrument
of repression was a vicious private army, the National Guard.
After the Triumph of the Revolution in July 1979, when the last
Somoza was overthrown, the hated National Guardsmen fled
across the borders into Honduras and Costa Rica. Here they re-
grouped and started the counter-revolution.

The Nicaraguan Revolution was fought and won by the
Sandinista Front for the Liberation of Nicaragua. In the two
years following the Triumph their achievements were staggering.
Over forty thousand landless rural families were given access to
land on which to grow food for the first time. Infant mortality
was reduced by one third, malaria was halved. Polio, measles
and tetanus were all but eradicated. Illiteracy in over half the
population was cut to less than one seventh. More than one
million Nicaraguans began receiving formal education in 1200
newly-built schools. Food production rose by 10 per cent,
consumption by 40 per cent.

In 1980 the regime in Washington changed. Jimmy Carter,
who had provided the Sandinista government with aid since
1979, was replaced by hard-liner Ronald Reagan. Reagan
immediately withdrew Carter's aid and imposed a crippling
embargo on all trade between the United States of America and
Nicaragua. He then went on to give military assistance to the
counter-revolutionary, or Contra, forces in Honduras. After

1981 the Contra war and Reagan's rhetoric gathered momentum. By 1984, when Nicaragua held its first free elections, one hundred million dollars' worth of military aid had been supplied by the US to the Contras, thirty thousand women, children and men had been mutilated and murdered, and four hundred health centres had been destroyed by Ronald Reagan's 'freedom fighters'. In 1986 it was revealed that a Marine Lieutenant-Colonel in the depths of the White House had been selling arms to Iran in exchange for the release of hostages and channelling the money to the Contras. The scandal of Oliver North and Contragate permeated right to the top of the Reagan Administration but failed to topple it. Indeed, in 1988 Reagan's vice-president George Bush followed him into the Oval Office.

Contragate aroused my interest in the plight of the Nicaraguan people. I was angered by the way Ronald Reagan had so blithely subverted the US democratic process in order as he saw it to hasten a 'democratic' solution to the problems of Central America. This after the Nicaraguans had contested the first free and fair elections in their history, abolished the death penalty and drawn up a constitution the like of which many in Britain are now calling for in order to safeguard our own battered democracy. My anger grew when I started to research a play on Nicaragua, and the scale of American injustice became apparent. In 1987 I wrote a play about the people who had most to gain from the Revolution but who were the principal victims of Ronald Reagan's war – the peasant farmers, or campesinos.

The Royal Shakespeare Company bought the production rights to the play, and after several revolutions of its own, including a change of title, it was premiered in September 1989. Roger Michell, who had previously directed two other plays of mine, *The Catch* for the Royal Court Theatre Upstairs and *The Dead Monkey* for the RSC, directed *Kissing The Pope*.

In the spring of 1988 Roger and I travelled to Nicaragua in order to aquaint ourselves with the subject matter of the play. The diary is an account of our trip.

Tuesday 26th April

Our journey took twenty hours. Roger had had the first night of his production of Vaclav Havel's *Temptation* the evening before so he slept longer than I did. We stopped over at San Domingo for an hour then on to Augusto C. Sandino airport, Managua. After a long haul through customs, our worst fears were confirmed: nobody to meet us. We had a letter of introduction to the Minister of Culture, but there was no telephone number. We sat for two hours on the concrete outside the airport lounge getting hotter and hotter and finally decided to take a taxi. The dilapidated Cadillac cost $30 for a 13 kilometre journey into Managua. The driver was speedy, and he swerved to avoid enormous potholes. At one point we veered to the left, just missing the carcass of a white bullock which lay stretched across the road. The stench of its rotting flesh followed us for a good half mile.

The Ministry of Culture had been Somoza's residence before the Triumph. A cool building, with tiled floors and plenty of shade. Nobody had heard of us. I asked if they'd phone the ASTC, the Cultural Workers' Union. They had heard of us and sent somebody to meet us who, as it happened, had seen us on the concrete and mistaken us for coffee-pickers. She'd expected RSC representatives to be wearing a collar and tie. We were picked up and driven to a hotelito for ASTC guests only. So here we are with two Cuban acrobats teaching circus skills, a Philippino photographer and a Russian translator named Boris whose version of *The Cherry Orchard* is currently playing here at Managua.

The hotelito is a single-storey building which stands on the edge of a park. Today the park was dedicated to a young US engineer and unicyclist called Ben Linder, who was murdered by the Contras a year ago. He is remembered with affection by the Nicaraguan people, and at 4.30pm the park was filled with jugglers, unicyclists, acrobats, a salsa band and children performing traditional animal dances with exotic masks. President Daniel Ortega drew up in a Landcruiser and sauntered over to the naming ceremony. Henceforth this place will be known as Ben Linder Park.

Linder's father spoke, and Ortega said a few words then wandered over to watch the children dancing. After a minute or two he walked back to his vehicle and drove away. Roger and I were astonished at the ease with which the Head of State moved amongst the people. Ortega is no Castro. Charisma is not his strong point. It's a stroke of Nicaraguan genius to have embodied the values of the Revolution not in their living leaders but in the martyred Sandino, who was assassinated by the first Somoza in 1934 and after whom the Sandinistas took their name. (His silhouette is on walls everywhere.) Sandino is the great unassailable legend of Nicaragua, and he's dead. Though Ortega's credentials are impeccable (he spent many years in jail tortured by Somoza's National Guard, and he fought heroically for the liberation of his country), he is Sandino's humble representative and casually accepted as one of the people.

6.15 pm. Dusk, pink light, cicadas, palms, unbearable heat.

Wednesday 27th April

It's too expensive to hire a car. We walked two miles through the heat to the Hotel Intercontinental to discover this. Then walked back, dehydrated and with one hat between us. Failure to wear a hat in this climate is to scorn the power of the sun.

Went to ASTC to discuss with Noel Carreras our game plan.

The ASTC, our host, is the Association of Cultural Workers, or the artists' union. It is headed by Rosario Murillo, who is one of Nicaragua's leading poets and Daniel Ortega's partner. The Association's headquarters, a stone's throw across the park from the hotelito, is a complex of single-storey buildings strewn like pearls amongst a lush garden of palms and dense greenery. There's a dance studio, offices, a cool bar/restaurant and a large outdoor area for concerts, usually given at night by local and international artistes. The policy of the Sandinistas is to introduce alternatives to the US dominated beefburger/baseball/gum society and steer the people towards a rediscovery of their own culture – or should I say discovery – it's hard to imagine the effect a revolution can have on a deprived population. Nobody knew the names of the trees or mountains before 1979, because there was no reason for learning them. The trees and mountains and everything else were the property of Somoza, whose power was so complete that he made no pretence of sharing his country with the people who lived there. They existed in a limbo-land which was itself out of bounds, beyond their reach.

Noel Carreras looks and behaves like a New Yorker, which is where he's lived much of his life. He's attached us to a US delegation who are arriving on Friday. We will travel with them. Meanwhile Roger and I have appended ourselves to a Philippino photographer, Rick, a big man with a face like the moon. Rick has an ASTC car and driver. This afternoon he took us round Managua.

Managua is the capital city of Nicaragua. In 1972 its centre was completely flattened by an earthquake. The international aid which poured in was embezzled by Somoza, and Managua stayed flat. Now, the closer you drive to the centre of town, the more barren it becomes, until you reach the middle, a desert overlooked by the Intercontinental Hotel, which along with the Bank of America was the only building to withstand the 'quake.

Rick had to photograph a children's diarrhoea ward in the hospital. The eradication of diarrhoea was one of the Revolution's great achievements. But the Contra war has eaten away at the country's medical resources, and, thanks to the efforts of Ronald Reagan, diarrhoea has once again climbed the charts to be the nation's number one killer. In a large blue room a dozen mothers sat on a bench holding their inert, underweight children. Now and again, a child would retch, but mostly they stared blankly across their mothers' shoulders at the wall. I fell into conversation (in Spanish) with one woman who talked non-stop about her child, his age, his weight, and the effects diarrhoea had on him.

Rick dropped us off at the Place de la Revolution. We had a quick look round then a short stroll to the Reuben Dario Theatre. Reuben Dario was Nicaragua's greatest poet, and the theatre which bears his name is a civic monolith. This is where *The Cherry Orchard* is playing, apparently to half empty houses, having been greeted with incomprehension by the critics. Noel had arranged for the director to meet us. She didn't. Too busy. So, a wasted journey and a long walk back to the hotelito at dusk. Pink light, cicadas etc. Four beers cost six quid.

We had our clothes laundered today, and ironed.

Thursday 28th April

6am. Retired early last night and rose at
4.30am. I'm beginning to despise this hotel. It makes me a
tourist, and that's the last sensation I want. If I can't get to share
even a particle of what it's like to be an ordinary citizen of
Nicaragua, then the visit is a sham. This hotel has
everything – air-conditioning, three square meals a day, yes
three, and very square: beans, rice and meat or fried cheese,
chicken. There's a swimming pool (piscina), shower, flushing
toilet; we could be on the Costa Blanca except it's too hot for
that and the whole thing's costing us $35 a day. However, Rick
introduced us last night to a carpenter who's lived all his life in
San Francisco but has returned to Nicaragua to help build a
school in Acoyapa. His name is Don Paco, and he looks like
Spike Milligan. His English is patchy despite a thirty-year
sojourn in the US. He's going to take us with him to Acoyapa,
heavy Contra territory south-east of Managua, and we'll stay
there two days – no beds, no latrines, nothing. So we'll soon be
getting dirty.

Rick, who is here at the behest of the ASTC to take
consciousness-raising publicity photographs, told us he is not,
remarkably, a professional photographer. He sells drugs – the
medicinal kind – and the most he's ever made taking pictures is
$75. He displays a generosity of time and spirit, not to mention
material sacrifice which would be hard to find in England. Here
is a man with no parsimonious patronage of the poor but real
empathy and concern, and who devotes every minute of his spare
time and every cent of his spare money to the cause. Is he a
saint? Of course not. Coming from where he does he sees the
world from a different perspective. In England charity is
replacing the state as the buffer against poverty, and yet we still
believe a small donation now and again will eradicate suffering.
Over here you get a full picture which demands not charity but a
commitment to change the world.

Friday 29th April

I've taken to writing this early (5.15am) in
bed. The air-conditioning, though effective, sounds like a DC10,
and every now and again it gets an automatic boost, which gives
the impression we're about to take off. Once you've woken it's
impossible to get back to sleep. I'll go for a swim . . . I'm now
away from the air-conditioning and sitting in the bowels of God's
own central-heating system.

A word about status. The more important they consider you,
the more you can expect from them. An international artist of
the Pinter/Rushdie calibre will get the five-star itinerary, i.e. a
driver and car. Another determinant of status is numbers. There
are eight Americans arriving today, and they will get to go round
in an air-conditioned bus. Roger and I comply with neither of
the above classifications and so enjoy nil status. Yesterday Noel
had promised us a driver to take us to the market in the
morning. We arrived at the ASTC. No car. No driver. No Noel.
Under any other circumstances, Noel would owe us a lot of
favours but in a country where so little is possible, yet so much is
achieved, isn't it natural to promise the earth in the hope that
maybe you can deliver a grain of sand?

So once again it was Rick who came to the rescue and took us
to the market. There are several markets in Managua, but this
one is the biggest. It stands on its own out of town, covers a vast
acreage and is housed in enormous hangar-like buildings. Small
recessed shops spill their goods out onto wide concourses. All
kinds of stuff is on sale, notably shoes. There are few imports.
The heat, of course, was unbearable. The sensation which hit me
and made the occasion unlike any other was not the size and
colour of the fruit nor the high artistic merit of the craftwork or
the mind-blowing, tropical, Dickensian scene of an army of
women making tortillas in engine-room heat over vast furnaces
fuelled with wood nor the noises of kids shouting nor the
incessant ringing of ice-cream vendors' bells nor the deep
ominous grinding of huge mince machines crushing mangoes,
the twitter of pullets in wicker baskets, the flapping of sandals on
the tiled floors, the whirr of home-made skateboards nor the
clumping of square-wheeled carts, nor even the sight of the
deformed, the legless, the very poor – the one thing that assured
me I could never be anything but an observer of this scene was
the smell. The smell of the meat in the butchery sector clung to

my nostrils, the odour of cheese in giant vats made me nauseous. The heat sits on a smell and squeezes it inwards through the pores of your skin. Everything you touch and eat, even the water you drink is charged with the smells of the market. Pungent and unfamiliar.

Roger and I visited the Museum of the Revolution, which is close by. Here the history of the armed struggle for the liberation of Nicaragua is laid out behind glass in the form of photographs, documents, the makeshift weapons used – bazookas made from drainpipes – and most potent, the clothes of the heroes. Sandino's leather jacket with a crudely mended rip on the hem is draped round a mannequin, and there beside it is a photo of the great man wearing the same jacket. This place is not the Imperial War Museum but a shrine with great emotional force, which is tangible like the smell in the market. When Ronald Reagan invaded Grenada, the Nicaraguans packed the exhibits up and buried them, so that if Reagan invaded Nicaragua next, which many thought he might, he couldn't destroy its history.

Rick is our friend and benefactor. He has another trip to a theatre this evening, a small fringe-group which I'm going to watch tonight with Don Paco the carpenter from San Francisco. Roger and I, who spent this morning like a couple of newly-weds, politely discussing money and trying on hats in the market, decide to take a rest from one another. He goes off with Rick, and I stay home to siesta. At four o'clock Roger comes bounding back. 'I've struck gold, mate.' And so he has. He's arranged a trip for us on Sunday, Labour Day, to go with the fringe theatre group to the Matagalpa region, where they will be taking part in the Mayday celebration, entertaining the troops in the war zone.

Tonight, Don Paco and his friend Gonzalo picked me up at dead on six and drove me through the gathering dusk and crazed, half-tamed anarchy which are the streets of Managua to the Teatro Justino Ruffino Garay. I swear to you this place is like the Bush, one of London's scruffiest but most go-ahead fringe theatres, but transported to Acacia Avenue in a deranged, tropical Orpington. The auditorium, seating and stage are identical to the Bush. The director, with her warm greeting and efficient charm, is the spitting-image of Jenny Topper, the Bush's artistic director. A woman queuing for a ticket carried a Boots the Chemist bag, and the two plays on offer were classic Bush fare, one-woman pieces by Dario Fo.

Whilst I was at the Bush, Roger returned to the Reuben Dario to sit in with Rosario Murillo and some musicians who were auditioning acts for ASTC. Finally we went to the ASTC to catch a local band called Praxis – jazz-funk fusion with more than a hint of Santana.

Observations: at the market I had my first (and only) experience of feeling threatened. A large drunk teetered over to me and, breathing sweet alcohol fumes in my face, demanded money. Having none, I backed off and ran. Later, I took the tape-recorder with me to the Bush and asked Don Paco and Gonzalo, could I leave it in the car? No way. The car would be broken into and vandalised. I found this difficult to believe, but it must be remembered that Don Paco and Gonzalo have spent most of their time in San Francisco.

There are slogans everywhere. Banners, Sandino silhouettes stencilled onto walls, stickers on trees, all with a political message. The favourite right now is 'We are flexible because we are strong'. This refers to the unpopular talks which are taking place between the Sandinistas and the leadership of the Contras, Enriquez Bermudez and Adolfo Calero. The Sandinistas swore they'd never do business with the Contras, but diplomatically the talks are vital, hence the slogan.

There's Beatles music everywhere.

Many women are pregnant.

I re-read my play. How can I square this odd piece with the momentousness around me? Is it true? Is it real? How can I absorb what I see and hear (and smell) into the text, and if I succeed will it make the play any more real? The most I can expect from this visit is to provide the play with a setting, a context. The characters come from within me, of course, and in one sense I'm looking for affirmation that the kind of people I write about exist in Nicaragua. I come from a remote rural area myself, and the play is about farmers. In the same way that I met Jenny Topper's counterpart earlier, I'm confident that a farmer is a farmer, wherever he or she might live.

Saturday 30th April

Our first trip out of Managua, courtesy of Rick. A short shoot north to Masaya by way of the volcano. We stood on the lip and looked down into a sulphurous smoking hole to the centre of the earth, down which Somoza used to drop Sandinista prisoners out of helicopters supplied by the USA. Charming man. An example of his philanthropy: after the earthquake, thousands needed blood. The call went out, and plasma was given by donors from all over the world, collected and delivered by the aid organisations to Managua airport. There it sat. The blood was requisitioned by Somoza and *sold* by him to the earthquake victims, his fellow-Nicaraguans.

Masaya is an old Spanish-colonial town, and one of the first to be liberated from Somoza's clutch. There were vendors in the market who didn't want to be photographed by Rick. It was the first example of camera-hostility he'd come across.

Rick had an assignment way off the beaten track in a tiny *barrio*, the inhabitants of which were all involved in spinning string from jute. Two huge sows lolled beside three old men and a youth, who teased the bundles of the coarse fibre into threads by thrashing it against a table of nails. The spinning technique is similar to that used by the rope-makers of Chatham and Bridport, several threads a hundred feet long are trained along pylons and spun together by an enormous wheel. Roger and I were mesmerised by the scene – one of serene tranquillity broken by the furious spinning of wheels. We recorded the sound they made. Recorded also is our reaction to Eujelio's driving, which is fast.

At the ASTC tonight there was a band called Moncatal, fronted by Luis Enriquez Mejia, one of the most charismatic performers I've ever seen. His music is Latin, salsa, exhilarating stuff. Before the Triumph he broadcast his revolutionary songs across the border from a radio station in Costa Rica. Now he's big right across north and south America. After him, a muscle-bound French version of Tom Jones. Machismo personified. Very popular.

Off afterwards with Matthew, the local Reuter's correspondent. His house, a mansion in the Orpington millionaire's row, is rented from an exiled Somocista. Two other journalists both American, greeted us round the pool. Scott, who writes for the *Christian Science Weekly*, and Charlie, who writes for the *Financial Times* in London. After a quick glass of delicious Nicaraguan rum, we head off to Charlie's place where he's entertaining tonight. This is a full-blown party we've stumbled on here. Roger and I sample what's on offer. Guests: Maria, an Algerian, and an unbearably vain Belgian TV journalist. Plus several of Scott's girlfriends, past, present and future. His life is complicated right now, which is perhaps why he offered to take us home at 12.30.

The journalists say there is no corruption (drugs, etc.) in this country. It doesn't surprise me to hear this; what does surprise me is to hear hard-bitten journalists tell me there is none. They also say that Nicaragua is the best place to be posted. I've got a speech of Scott on tape where he tells us that Nicaraguans stand out a mile from other Central Americans because of their liberated souls.

Monday 2nd May

5.15pm. Just got back. Extraordinary two days. Slept last night in ammo dump. Nearly killed on journey back.

I'll start on Sunday morning. Yesterday. May Day. The plan was to meet up at the theatre at 8.30am and away to Muy-Muy with a band to entertain the troops, then back in Managua by nightfall. Rick got us to the theatre on time, where we met the company, Claudia and Otie, whom I'd seen on Saturday night in the Fo plays, and a younger boy and girl of about eighteen. There was also a Dane called Martin, who was fluent in Spanish and English. Martin warned us that if our transport turned out to be an East German EFI truck we'd be lucky to get back alive because they tend to turn over. After waiting around for four hours – it was now noon – I was relieved to see they'd sent a bigger, Russian vehicle. We clambered up over the tailgate and sat on the flimsy wooden benches which ran the length of the truck's flat bed. After a further four hours travelling north, we turned off the main highway at Matagalpa onto a mountain grit-road which soon petered off into nothing more than a track through uninhabited bush. The military are trained to drive fast to avoid ambush. Our speed was a constant 90 kilometres an hour. It shook the shit out of me.

We arrived at Muy-Muy at dusk. The first sign of civilisation was a hillside covered with small fires like a scene from *Henry V*. We came to rest beside an empty parade ground surrounded by chicken-wire fencing. At the far end was a narrow stage with a wall behind it. The wall was pock-marked with bullet holes like the streets of Masaya. Portraits of Sandino and Fonseca were painted on the wall and flanked by black and red Sandinista flags. Flags flew everywhere round the square, high on bamboo poles. We were led through a thick plantation of jacarandas, mangoes and palm trees with their trunks painted black and red. Bullfrogs belched a greeting. We came to an enormous piscina fed with water from a pipe high up like a waterfall. This place had been the weekend retreat of a high-ranking Somocista.

Campesinos had travelled from all over Nicaragua to be with the soldiers, who had come down from patrolling the mountains for the first time in a year. Roger, Rick, Martin and I were the only 'Internationalistas' amongst a thousand soldiers and their families, deep in the war zone. The band went off to prepare for their gig. We knelt at the pool and washed the dust off our faces. We were so hot we stripped and bathed.

We ate beans and rice and drank rum at a long table with twenty soldiers. One soldier leaned over and introduced himself. He spoke quietly. Martin interpreted. His name was Carlos. He was the political cadre of the platoon. He told us about the war with the Contras, how it is fought and why. He talked intensely for three-quarters of an hour, articulating with a measured fervour. I put his age at thirty, but it turned out he was nineteen years old and a sub-lieutenant. He'd been a soldier for five years and had fought for the Revolution since he was eight. He put us entirely at ease in this extraordinary place.

Carlos took us back to the parade ground, which was now crammed with people, then vanished. Claudia and Otie taught Roger and I how to salsa. I'm a good dancer and Roger is light on his feet, but I'm not sure how successful we were with the salsa. The movement derives from the hip, which Englishmen often find hard to dislodge from the perpendicular. Looking round I witnessed a scene of joyful abandonment. Rivers of rum had been consumed, but I heard no breaking glass; there was no hint of aggression. These soldiers were nothing more than kids having a rare night out with their families. There were children of all ages, but those aged fourteen and over were in uniform: the pale-yellow tee-shirt, camouflage trousers, red bandana, sweatband round the head and the distinctive soft jungle hat worn with pride by the crack BLI regiment. Tomorrow they'd be back in the mountains with their Kalashnikovs.

We danced till midnight, then it rained: a light shower, but it emptied the square and the band ceased playing. It was the first rain of the season, and the smell from the ground was overpowering.

We were ushered into a 15ft × 10ft store with four slatted shelves either side about 4ft deep. The room was full of semiautomatics and ammo. There were two false legs leaning against the wall, and it wasn't until we tried to go to bed that we discovered their owners asleep on two of the shelves. Eight of us slept here. I had two belts of live ammunition for a pillow; and Roger nestled up to a rocket-launcher. Rick snored very loud throughout the night, an extraordinary snore which started soft and built slowly to a deafening crescendo. I recorded it.

I set foot outside at dawn and was met with the sight of campesinos asleep everywhere. At one place I counted seven hammocks slung one above the other between two trees. Knots of men scuffed dirt round burros, while women collected water in bright-coloured plastic buckets. There was one latrine that I could see which served a thousand people. It was a hole in the ground surrounded by a box. The hole was full of shit and the box was full of flies so I made my way down the hillside and squatted. At a moment when it would have been impossible to stand up and pretend I was doing something else a campesino family filed past me and squatted in a line about ten feet further down the hill. There was mother, father and five kids. The scene took on a religous quality as we all faced east and watched the sun rise together, shitting in concert.

Roger spoke at length to the paraplegics who'd lost their legs stepping on land-mines. They'd been treated like heroes since their discharge from active service. They were now at Managua University, studying to be engineers.

At twelve noon we were ushered into a massive ten-wheeler. This time we had two spare wheels and a fifty gallon drum full of oil in the back. The truck filled with campesinos going home. Before long it was full to capacity. Roger and I were near the front, he had his back to the cab and I leaned against a single wooden rail which bowed out every time we went round a corner. Sitting on a spare wheel in front of me was a campesina of about sixty, thin and mischievous. She provoked the trumpet player into a relentless squabble by saying things like, 'All musicians smoke marijuana', or 'Daniel Ortega has four swimming pools and a Cadillac', which sent the trumpet player wild. Then she said, 'Soon this country will be full of old people, they're killing all the young ones'. She spoke with a smile and kept glancing at me as if to say, 'Watch how he reacts to this one'. Then out of the blue she roared, 'All Internationalistas bring AIDS to Nicaragua'. This time she was denounced as a *La Prensa* reader. *La Prensa* is the CIA backed pro-Contra newspaper which peddles misinformation and does its best to undermine the Sandinistas.

The driver of this truck was a maniac. His foot never left the cab floor. His homicidal tendencies reached their nadir when we were hurtling down a mountainside at 80 kph and swung out to negotiate a right-hander at the bottom. He swerved to avoid another vehicle coming up. The truck lurched hideously to the right, we were thrown about like dolls in the back and the fifty-gallon drum tottered over into Rick. Then the driver swerved to correct the skid, and we lurched as far in the other direction. By a miracle we survived. First there were screams, then yells of abuse at the driver. 'You'll kill us all!' 'Are you trying to do the Contras' job for them!' If he showed any sign of recklessness for the rest of the journey, the driver would get a torrent of catcalls from the back. The closest to death I've ever been.

Tuesday 3rd May

Don Paco and Gonzalo picked us up at 6.30am sharp, and we travelled to Acoyapa. Gonzalo is an aggressive driver too, and we had 200 kilometres of hell. Don Paco is involved with the San Francisco Bay Area Solidarity Group, which is building a school and workshops down here. Bill, also a carpenter like Don Paco, had just driven a Toyota flatbed loaded with tools down the pan-American highway from California to Nicaragua. Bill had given US customs false documents and a destination in Costa Rica, as it would be embargo-busting for the tools to wind up in Nicaragua. Bill is an artisan, retired. A solid, thoughtful man. He told us that, thanks to the military, driving through Guatemala and El Salvador is a death-defying act. It's well-known everywhere outside the White House that these two countries are controlled by their armies, which are corrupt and murderous. In making the journey, Bill ran the risk of having his throat cut and his truck stolen by the US-backed forces of democracy in Central America.

Acoyapa is a town the size of Padstow in Cornwall, and it has a full-size baseball stadium. The home team was hosting a league series, so Roger and I got to see our first match. The standard of play seemed very high. Bill informed us the game is a legacy left by the American Marines who occupied Nicaragua in the twenties and thirties before Sandino booted them out. 'That's the way we have of doing things,' said Bill. 'We come into a country and introduce the children to baseball while we're out killing their moms and dads.' Everywhere you go in Nicaragua there's a kid wielding a baseball bat.

The school is a single room, 30ft × 20ft, with concrete walls to waist height then open to the roof. About fifty kids of all ages sat at tables facing the teacher. There was no evidence of books, however the children had satchels and exercise books, though there is a shortage of pencils. The uniform is a starched white shirt and skirt or trousers. Schools and teachers are prime targets. Ronald Reagan knows that knowledge is power, and his freedom fighters are trained to destroy school buildings and to rape and murder staff as a disincentive to taking on the job.

Roger said it's hard to keep sight of the play in these surroundings. I can see what he means but it isn't him who has to re-write it. How much of the play squares with what I'm experiencing now and how much is inaccurate? In the first scene a brigadista (health worker) arrives at the village and takes blood samples from everyone who has had contact with pesticides. She then proceeds to demonstrate how to use protective clothing provided by the ministry. Thanks to Mr. Reagan there is a shortage of protective clothing in Nicaragua, and there are no longer the medical supplies to test blood for toxin levels. Would it be correct of me to imply that the medical supplies are holding up or better to scrap that scene and write another which deplores the lack of these resources? In the second scene we move to the undergrowth away from the village, where the Contras have re-grouped after attacking the village at the end of scene one. They have captured a youth of fifteen, Emilio, his father and the brigadista. The man is mutilated then murdered before his son's eyes, and when the Sandinista army mounts a counter-offensive the brigadista escapes. The play then proceeds on a dual-track, leap-frogging from the village to the camp where Emilio has been taken to be trained as a Contra. When Max Stafford-Clark did a rehearsed reading of the play with the *Serious Money* cast in the Royal Court's Theatre Upstairs, the most successful scenes were the murder scene and the ones with Emilio and his wild captor, Sanchez. The problem with the village scenes is the central character of Emilio's mother, Rosa, who has just suffered the double tragedy of a murdered husband and kidnapped son. Grief is hard to write in a cynical age. Synge managed it in *Riders to the Sea*, but in his time an audience's emotional response would have been stronger and less hedged. Besides, Synge used the device of keening, which is a formal expression of mourning and a technique not at my disposal. Grief is a mixture of emotions – not just mourning but a fear for the future, repugnance for the murderers, a desire for revenge, all of which are complicated in my character's case because her son is in mortal danger and there's a helplessness arising from that. I cannot have her speak this, or show it in the way she behaves. But any action which occurs in the village, such as the trial of a captured Contra or the re-building of the CDS (Sandinista Defence Committee) hut, and which doesn't place her centre stage appears thoughtless. She is a sponge to soak up the tragedy. Squeeze her and what comes out? Soap.

We stayed a few hours in Acoyapa but had to leave by mid-afternoon as the roads here are sealed off at dusk because of Contra activity.

Don Paco treated us to a meal at Nicaragua's most famous fish restaurant, which is nowhere near the sea or the lake. We ate the most expensive and delicate fish, which resembled a gurnard and tasted like cod.

Thursday 5th May

The Americans are here, and we now have the choice of attaching ourselves to them or continuing with Rick. They're off for two days, one of which will be spent on a co-operative farm, so I plump to travel with them. Our first stop, however, is at a Bulgarian canning plant stuck out on the plains just north of Managua. This monstrosity, straight out of a Herzog movie, is foreign aid on a grand scale. The Bulgarians have built a factory capable of peeling, washing, boiling, processing, pickling, canning, labelling and packing millions of tomatoes an hour. However the Nicaraguans can provide neither the tomatoes, the labour to pick them, the seeds to grow them, the trucks to transport them, the fuel for the trucks if they had them nor the electricity to power the plant. They will one day, when the war is over and the trade embargo is lifted, but until then the place stands silent, with thousands of gleaming empty cans on motionless conveyor belts. The union official who showed us round was full of pride for the place, empty as it was.

There are six women and two men in the delegation, here to prove to the Nicaraguans that not all Americans are redneck commie-haters. Each member had a present for the guide which was given with messages of goodwill for the workforce and the Nicaraguan people from the citizens of the country which is doing its best to destroy theirs. Their tone when they talk of Ronald Reagan is one of a parent apologising for an unruly child. I must say I was apprehensive about travelling with the Americans. At least with Rick you're with somebody who's doing a job of work which is of benefit to the country, but with the Americans I felt more like a tourist than I did before. This feeling was compounded during our guided tour of the cannery, but dispelled for ever after our next visit.

In Matagalpa we were taken to meet the Mothers of the Heroes and Martyrs. About one hundred and fifty women of all ages and their children. We entered the crowded hall and were applauded. No attempt was made to silence the meeting. Silence is a product of repression, and the lack of it is a mark of the Revolution's success. We sat opposite the Mothers behind a long table.

The jefa (leader) stood first and said, 'In the name of all the mothers, welcome. All here have lost children. Sometimes the women can't speak because it is too hard and emotional and they'd be too upset to talk about it. This lady has lost all her beloved family including her husband and children. She's the only one that remains.' The woman in question stood up to be shown, then sat down again. Then Karmen spoke. Karmen is a civil rights lawyer from L.A., and this is her eighth trip as delegation leader. She interpreted both ways. She gave her name and said she was from Ventura, California. One by one the delegation members introduced themselves until finally I stood and gave my name. 'I'm from London England; our prime minister, Margaret Thatcher, supports Ronald Reagan's policies, but there are millions of ordinary people in Great Britain who do not support Margaret Thatcher.' Of course the mothers had never heard of England nor Margaret Thatcher, to them I was an American and that's what mattered. There was a hiatus, then a mother rose and said, 'When the Contras have killed your sons, it's not easy to repeat what happened, how they were killed, but we think, if we tell you, you will denounce it when you return to your country.' Another woman said, 'In Nicaragua although we are very poor nobody dies of hunger. We have been hearing that in your country people have been dying of cold and starvation. The campesino children here have a chance to go to university, and that's the result of our struggle.' Catha, the youngest delegation member, stood and spoke in halting Spanish. 'I'm a student from Los Angeles, and I'm very heartened to hear what the mother said about the children of campesinos getting to university. I think your health and literacy campaigns are a model to the world, and when I get back to the States I'm certainly going to tell them about the courage of you people here. I'm ashamed to be an American, and if I could lay down my life for you like so many of your children have I would gladly lay down my . . .' Here she had to stop, overcome with emotion. The mothers applauded her. After several more speeches, a mother stood up. She was about forty and frail. She wore a tee-shirt with a picture of the Pope on the front. 'Would you tell the student not to cry? She has to be strong like us. It's the only way we'll win, through strength and solidarity. We are thankful that you people are here today; it means so much to us. We hope that you will go back and show your solidarity to Ronald Reagan.' I had the impression throughout the meeting that the mothers expected us to tell Ronald Reagan personally to get his ass out of Nicaragua. Of course this is a country where it's possible to do that with your president. Once a week Daniel Ortega goes to a barrio for a gruelling (and televised) 'Face the People', when for up to three hours he fields questions and brickbats direct from the electorate. The meeting with the mothers was moving, and it brought home to me how vital it is for a bunch of ordinary Americans to express solidarity with the victims of their leader's murderous policies, however remote they might be from his ear.

That night we stayed in a hotel way up in the mountains close to the border. Here were monkeys and parrots and big insects. I caught one for my son Henry. The beast was too fat for a matchbox, so I emptied a box of sticking plasters and put it in that. This I placed in the padded pocket of my camera bag.

The co-operative farm was the highlight of my trip. This is where I would get the perspective I needed to give edge to the play, since it is set on just such a farm. The president, Miguel, showed us round. The place was primitive. He showed us a plough carved from the branch of a tree. The share was a plate of steel bolted to the front. This would be pulled by two oxen. The only other tool was the omnipresent machete. Of course they use pesticides. Do they wear protective clothing? 'We don't have it'. We saw a mountain side being cleared for cultivation. I asked Miguel what they planned growing here. 'Potatoes, beetroots, carrots, coffee.' The co-operative functions democratically, so a campesino who wants to join will propose himself, and the members have a meeting to discuss whether they should let him join or not.

'Would you ever turn a person away?'

'If we know somebody's a drunk and not likely to work, we won't let that person join.'

'What about an ex-Contra, would he get in?'

'There have been counter-revolutionaries who have asked to join certain co-operatives, and they've been let in. Under the law of amnesty any Contra who was a campesino before he was a Contra is entitled to land.'

The qualification here is important. Many Contras are unwilling abductees from farms, taken across the border and trained by CIA advisors. When these Contras escape or are captured, they get amnesty, but there is a distinction to be made between this kind of Contra and the hardened ex-national guardsman who would be ideologically committed to the destruction of the Revolution. These are incarcerated in an open prison (few bother to escape) taught a trade and rehabilitated slowly for their own good as much as society's, because they are despised by the Nicaraguans.

'What other officials are there besides the president?'

'There are those responsible for production, organisation, education, defence and finance. They are all elected at a meeting of the whole co-operative. Everybody has a vote. The co-operative is self-governing. We make all our own decisions.'

'How often are the officers elected?'

'It depends. If you have someone in office who's not doing their job you replace them.'

'How?'

'We have a meeting and say, we are going to replace you.'

'This is an ordinary campesino, who will tell someone to their face?'

'Of course.'

'Why are people dismissed?'

'It's not as though they're doing anything wrong. They just weren't performing up to capacity. Like if they're late with plans. Everybody has to co-ordinate the harvests, and if they're late with the plans they're not going to comply with their job responsibilities. It's not as if they're grasping or corrupt.'

The co-operative had a small schoolroom. Miguel showed us inside his house, which had two rooms with an oven in one corner. There was a bench to sit on and a hammock slung across the main room. That's all there was in the way of furniture. No ornaments. Outside, a rocking chair. There were barbed wire washing lines across the square in front of the co-operative's meeting hut, and against one wall there was a single tap over a stone basin. A spruce woman with her hair tied tight back in a bun was washing beans. Her fingernails were painted with red varnish.

I spoke at length with two old campesinos, who were leaning over the balcony of the hut waiting for a lift to Jinotega. I knew these characters well. I've met a thousand like them in the Molesworth Arms, Wadebridge, on a market day. I'm not here to find characters for my play. The most common question I'm asked as a playwright is, 'Who did you base such-and-such a character on?' and it's a mis-question because the answer is no one. No one character is based on a single human being. All characters are composites of many people the author might know intimately or hardly at all. The nuts and bolts of a character are the common roots of all humanity. Scratch a Nicaraguan farmer and a Cornish farmer and you'll find the only difference between them is the width of their hat brims.

Inside the hut was a consignment of wellington boots from Russia. Outside was a rusty fifty gallon drum of DDT – from Surrey, England.

Friday 6th May

We spent the morning in the company of a Miskito Indian representative from the Atlantic Coast. There are about 500,000 inhabitants in the eastern half of the country, which is more or less cut off from the west. The language and culture of the Indians are different, and Somoza didn't bother with them. As a result the Triumph didn't mean much to them, and when the Sandinistas tried to coerce them into the Revolution, the results were a disaster. The Indians' leader, one Steadman Fagoth, joined the Contras, and many Miskitos fled across the border to Honduras. However the Sandinistas have admitted their mistakes and have ceded to the Miskito demands for autonomy.

Then on to the Ministry for Internal Affairs and a meeting with a charming civil servant, who told us plenty but not much we didn't know already. In the afternoon Roger and the Americans went to the dollar store. Karmen's friend Laura came over to the hotelito. Laura is a sociologist working for the Ministry of Agriculture and the University. She's spent the last five years studying the effect of agrarian reform on the campesinos. I asked her if I could come tomorrow to visit a group of independent farmers, but she said no, they're sensitive to outsiders. Apparently a few of these farmers have to fiddle their quotas to get by, and they are suspicious of strangers.

It's 11.30pm. Roger and I have been talking to a woman we've seen round the hotelito but never spoken to. Her name is Herita Stern, she's a theatre worker and a famous TV actress in her native Uruguay. She teaches theatre to actors in the eight theatre groups in the Nicaraguan Army. She did *Romeo and Juliet* and two scenes from *Macbeth*, the murder of Duncan and the handwashing scene. The significance of *R & J* is obvious given the average age in the army is seventeen. The explanation for doing the *Macbeth* scenes is to dramatise the treachery in the Contra camps between Bermudez (Macbeth) and Calero (Duncan). Herita's husband was thirteen years in a Uruguayan gaol, and she herself was a political prisoner for six. She said while she was in gaol she had her identity stripped from her. Her hair was cropped short and she was known only by a number and a colour. To keep sane she and her fellow prisoners formed a clandestine theatre group. Of course they were allowed no texts, but, having been an actress and director, Herita found she could remember whole plays. When they didn't know the words they made them up. They gave performances of Lorca and Strindberg to secret gatherings. She had spent a lifetime in theatre and TV in Uruguay, rising to stardom and playing in anything that made her money before she realised that 'theatre does not exist unless it is a social or political act'. She knew no English, so she spoke Italian to Roger. It was novel having him interpret.

Saturday 7th May

5.30pm. Today was our first day with absolutely bugger all to do. Rick and the Americans have gone and the place is empty without them. Roger and I took a walk

over to the ASTC, and Marguerite (Noel's associate) was there
(Noel is in New York learning French). She was polite but
unhelpful. She said she might go to the beach on Sunday, and if
she does she'll take us with her. Bumped into Jose, a San
Dominican lawyer who has a responsible job with the New York
District Attorney. Jose quotes Shakespeare and Ogden Nash
whilst groping his girlfriend. He was off to the beach but despite
heavy hints from Roger he didn't offer us a lift. We tried
phoning some people we knew, but they must all be at the beach.
I lay on the bed all day reading. I couldn't even summon the
energy to write this diary. I slept a lot and began to think of
home. There are some people to whom travel is an imperative
and others for whom it is hell. I fall into the latter category.

My conviction that the play should be strictly about
campesinos is waning. Nicaragua is a young country,
inexperienced in everything except the art of war. Youth is a
vital ingredient of any play about Nicaragua. The greatest
concentration of youth here is in the army. So perforce the play
should be about the army. This would mean quite a serious re-
write. Roger shrugs when I mention this. I know Roger: a shrug
is a strongly affirmative act. He won't push me any more, but I
can see he's hinting at major re-writes. I steer him back to the
play. 'It has a cartoon quality which I like,' I say. No response.
'But the dual-plot structure would buckle if we loaded it with any
more material.' Roger nods, he agrees with that. Roger's keen
there should be a debate about the nature of democracy, and that
the problem of acute shortages of everything from toilet rolls to
tractors should feature. I'm quite happy to abandon the play as it
stands, but there's one scene which I think is too good to lose
and that's the murder scene. The one where Emilio has to watch
his father being killed. There is an American Civilian Military
Advisor in this scene, who orders the killing but doesn't carry it
out. That honour is left to Sanchez, the Contra who takes Emilio
back to Honduras. Sanchez doesn't know that the man he killed
is Emilio's father (neither does anyone incidentally, until Emilio
tells us at the end of the scene). Roger agrees with me that it's a
good scene and it has several bona fides. One, it's about youth;
two, it places the blame for the war squarely on the shoulders of
Uncle Sam.

Sunday 8th May

Laura came round with a paper on
'Agricultural Policy and the Campesino,' which she wanted
back, so I spent an hour dictating it into the tape-recorder.
Roger dropped heavy beach-hints, but she seemed to be the one
person in the whole of Managua who wasn't spending Sunday by
the sea.

After lunch Roger and I sparred with the play. We're both
agreed the murder scene should start the play, but that means
ditching the pesticides scene because it precedes it chronologically.
One could play with time and have the murder scene start the first
half of the play, tell the Honduras story straight through and then
go back to the village after the interval, starting with the pesticides
scene. This is how I wrote an earlier play, *The Body*; with great
effect.

The only Honduran scene I would fight for is the 'fat girl/thin
girl' scene. This takes place in the camp at night when Sanchez
has lined up two prostitutes for himself and Emilio. It's too good
a scene to jettison, but Roger asks what it's about. I'm not sure.
I think it's about the American Dream. This is not apparent to
Roger from the scene as it stands, and he suggests I elaborate it
along that line. This brings me on to Icaza. Icaza is the Contra
in charge of the political education of new recruits. When he was
directing the reading, Max Stafford-Clark had pointed out to me
that Icaza is the least successful character in the play, but I
hadn't been able to improve on him much at the time. When a
character doesn't sparkle for me, I have two choices: ditch him
or take him off-stage. This can be effective, and I can see ways of
mentioning him in the American Dream.

Roger hasn't said as much but I have a suspicion he's terrified
of the play turning into a worthy 'revolutionary tractor' story. I
have this fear too. Particularly if we overload the play with our
new material. The pressure on me to drop the campesino strand
altogether is becoming very great, and the attraction even
greater. Sanchez is the best character in the play, followed closely
by Emilio. Emilio is a good foil for Sanchez; they make a great
double-act. And I'm on home ground when I'm writing these
two because I have two sons of my own. They are both younger
than Sanchez and Emilio, but we are born with our emotional
equipment intact. Growing up is a matter of hiding and
controlling our feelings, and Emilio and Sanchez are still kids in

this respect, because they haven't acquired these adult tricks.

Talk of abandoning the campesino strand has filled me with guilt. I must not yet cast them into the wilderness.

After an early dinner I went back to reading. Roger interrupted me at eight, and we joined Boris, the Russian translator, and his wife, Irena, for a drink on the patio. After an uneventful day we spent a quiet evening communicating with these two soft-spoken Russians in broken English on glasnost, theatre, Sandino – practically everything under the sun. They were celebrating the Great Patriotic Victory – the end of the Second World War, in which twenty million of their fellow-countrymen died. We solemnly drank a toast to Winston Churchill, which apparently is something all Russians do on this day every year. Roger and I were anxious to talk about the changes which are happening behind the Iron Curtain, and they were keen to tell us. They are confident the Berlin Wall will be a memory by the end of the decade. I suggested that the end of the Cold War will be seen as a victory for the West and a vindication of all our posturing, and Irena took this to be my opinion. It's difficult to explain to someone with scant English that what you are saying is not what you believe yourself to be the truth, and I'm not sure I was entirely successful in clearing up the misunderstanding. I told them my play, *The Dead Monkey*, is at this moment being translated into Russian and a production is planned in 1990. So we agreed to meet in Leningrad.

Monday 9th May

7pm. Today we visited Alan
Bolt – Renaissance man: ecologist, agronomist, Marxist, dissident, playwright, producer, director, architect – at his hacienda north of Matagalpa in the most fertile region of Nicaragua. We talked for an hour in his wooden house, which reminds me of my place in Kent. Bolt's grandfather was an Englishman who made his fortune in Nicaragua from the railways. He took us round his estate of about eighteen manzanas (about 100 acres) and showed us his experiments in the cultivation of new fruits and vegetables, his erosion halting planting schemes, his non-chemical pesticides, and the bamboo

project. In this area alone they are going to have to build 50,000
new houses in the next five years. With the war and the
embargo, building materials are in short supply. To avoid
cutting down hardwood, Alan is experimenting with bamboo – it
grows fast, needs no seasoning, just curing, is flexible and
versatile. The A-frame living units Alan has built bear this out.
Everything from the floor joists to the roof is made of bamboo.
I'm envious at the ease with which the stuff grows here; I'd love
to be able to build a bamboo shed.

Alan's theatre group performed two rumbustious scenes from
one of his plays: much music and a cartoon-like depiction of
Nicaragua's tortured history. America is the villain of the piece.
The French and English come in for scrutiny, but after 1850 it's
Uncle Sam all the way, from Vanderbilt through the United
Fruit Company up to Reagan. 'Banana Republic' is a
derogatory term but it was the Americans who created the cash-
crop economy from which the name derives. Alan's company
tours the barrios and villages of Nicaragua with a repertoire of
three or four home-made plays. The actors are young and
vigorous, and I was left exhausted.

We travelled up with John Carlin, the correspondent for *The
Independent*, and his girlfriend, Maria, whose brother, a
Sandinista, was killed three months after the Triumph. She's
researching a book about the mystery surrounding his death.
Her family were all Somocistas except for her and her brother,
who were revolutionaries. The split family syndrome is a
common, tragic occurrence. And there was Abbie, who arranged
the trip. She had worked with film director Alex Cox on his
movie, *Walker*, and co-produced the Oscar Cabezas film, *Fire
From the Mountain*. When we set off from Managua in John's car,
I thought at last we'd get some sensible English driving, but
apparently journalists are trained to drive fast to get to the next
assignment. We reached Matagalpa in record time.

Tomorrow we fly home and I've been packing. I opened the
padded pocket of the camera bag and discovered that the beetle I
picked up for my son is alive. Not only that, it's managed to
scratch its way through the plaster box and halfway out of the
pocket. This beetle deserves its liberty. I took it out to Ben
Linder Park and released it. The park was empty and dark. It
was 11pm, and I recalled how busy the place had been on the
day of our arrival. I took a little walk around, probably treading
on the newly liberated beetle, and turned down the road, past
Ortega's house and onto the main highway into the centre of
town. I walked till gone midnight and then walked back. I had

no fear walking the streets of this capital city. When I returned to the hotelito, Roger had half a bottle of rum to finish and a couple of cans of coke, so we took them back to the park and drank them.

The question on everybody's lips is: why? Why us? Why is Ronald Reagan fighting this war? Why are we such a threat? Why does he hate us? Nobody seems to know the answer. There's no doubt that the Sandinistas are a force for good, not only in Nicaragua but in Central America. They have the interests of the ordinary people at heart. Everybody says this. I've not met one nun, one nurse, one priest, one teacher, one doctor, one campesino, one journalist who denies it. Yes, the Sandinistas are a threat to American business interests because now, instead of all profits from cash-crops such as cotton, coffee etc. flowing out of the country straight into US corporate banks, the money stays put in Nicaragua. US big business has plundered Central America for so long, maybe it feels it has a divine right to the region's wealth?

There's no doubt in anybody's mind who's fighting this war: Ronald Reagan. Whatever else the play says, it should say that. It should also show how cynical it is to have Nicaraguans fighting their own people. At least when Sandino was around, the Yanks had the honesty to put their own marines into combat. There's also no doubt that we are in a Catholic country, and, with three priests on the National Directorate, the Sandinistas can hardly be accused of propounding a 'godless creed'.

The play should begin with an atrocity (the murder) and end with a bright ray of hope. Ronald Reagan goes at the end of this year and his successor, even if it's George Bush, won't share his obsessive hatred of Sandismo. There's a ceasefire on at the moment, and talks with the Contras, but the trade embargo has to be lifted. Whoever said sanctions don't work should come to Nicaragua: the country is on its knees. Certainly the people's spirit has not been broken, but there's a relentlessness about Reagan's onslaught – political, economical and military – which will in time cause the Nicaraguans to shorten their vision and start blaming those closer to home for the appalling grind of everyday life. It's a young country, and when those who are not of an age to remember Somoza become the majority, Ronald Reagan's chickens will start to come home to roost.

The Pope also has a lot to answer for, I reckon. When he visited Managua recently on one of his tours, a member of the Sandinista National Directorate who's a priest (Ernesto Cardinale, I'm not sure) knelt to kiss the Pope's ring and the pontiff withdrew his hand. The Pope makes no secret of whose side he's on, and his attitude to the Sandinistas must make Catholics, devout and lapsed, despair.

Roger and I kicked the Pope about in Ben Linder Park into the small hours and discussed a title for the play, the new version which starts with the murder and tells the story of Emilio and Sanchez. *Kick the Pope*? Too abrasive. *Kiss the Pope* – that's better. Too short, needs another syllable. My mother used to say that Laurence Olivier was a successful actor because he had the right number of syllables in his name for people to remember it. *Kissing the Pope*. Maybe.

KISSING THE POPE

Author's note

The RSC production of *Kissing The Pope* was too long. This is no reflection on the excellent work that Roger Michell and the cast put into the play, but on my ability to see where to cut it. An audience is the best judge and I can tell after the first public performance where a play works and where the dead zones are. I've reduced the length of the first two scenes, shifted the interval back to before the fat girl/thin girl scene (now entitled 'American Dream'), and re-written scene four. I've also removed certain visual images which I thought would give an intense theatrical experience but in performance did not. I've given the central character, Sanchez, a more complex moral base by making him responsible for not only the death of Emilio's father but also that of the American at the end of scene one.

As I said in the diary, Nicaragua is a young country, and *Kissing The Pope* is a play about youth. In my view it is vital that the casting reflects this. Emilio and Sanchez are fifteen and eighteen years old respectively and they should be played by actors of that age. The only characters in the play who are over the age of twenty are Emilio's father and the American, Heck, who is old enough to have fought in Vietnam. And as it happens they both die in the first scene, after which we are left with two children struggling to rationalise a cruel and dangerous world. The intensity of sharing this experience with an audience is diminished if the children are played by two adult actors, however good they are (and in the RSC production they were the best).

Kissing the Pope was first staged in the Almeida Theatre Islington, London, by the Royal Shakespeare Company on 19 September 1989.

The cast was as follows:

HECK	Edward Peel
PEDRO	Jason Watkins
CASCABEL	Kevin Doyle
JULIO	Julia Tarnoky
LOUISA	Vivienne Rochester
SANCHEZ	Mark Hadfield
EMILIO	Christian Dixon
JOSUE	Jack James
CHICO	Paul Sykes
ECO	Dominic Rickhards
ALDO	Richard Bremmer
VULTURE	Jack James
SKINNY GIRL	Julia Tarnoky
PABLO	Paul Sykes
MIGUEL	Jack James
RICO	Kevin Doyle
JUANITA	Vivienne Rochester
HERNANDEZ	Richard Bremmer
EDWIN	Jason Watkins

Directed by Roger Michell
Designed by Eryl Ellis & Kenny MacLellan
Costumes by Allan Watkins

The play takes place in NICARAGUA and HONDURAS.

There is an intermission between scenes two and three.

Scene One

Nicaragua.
A farmhouse on Chachagua Mountain, close to the Honduran border. 12
*noon. Outside it is bright sunlight. The house serves as a forward base and
store for a Contra Unit.*

Three prisoners, LOUISA, ALDO *and* EMILIO *sit on the floor. They
are dirty, tired and frightened. They are guarded by* PEDRO, *a sullen
Contra of 25 who lies on the floor with a rucksack under his head, and a
FAL automatic rifle across his chest. He reads a dilapidated bible.
Scattered round the room are boxes of ammo, cigarettes, rum etc. In one
corner is a pile of tarpaulins, rucksacks and tents.*

> JOSUE, *a Contra, enters the house. Ignoring the prisoners he splits
> open a case of cigarettes, takes an armful of Chesterfield packets and
> standing in the doorway calls names, slinging packets of cigarettes out as
> he does so.*

JOSUE. Leon! Pollo! Curo! Caramalo! Pajara! Rodriguo!
Muerte! Eco!

> *Another Contra,* CHICANO, *his chest criss-crossed with ammo belts,
> elbows past* JOSUE *through the door, opens a case of Ron Plata (rum)
> and takes two bottles out with him.*

> JOSUE *exits with a carton of Chesterfields.*

> CASCABEL, *a Contra, enters and picks up a Patrolfine* SC – 130
> *radio. He takes it and places it on the balcony outside the window. He
> unfolds the antennae and slings them up on the roof, then clambers up
> after them. He can be heard walking about on the roof.*

> *Enter* HECK, *an American Civilian Military Advisor. A big man of
> about 40, he is dressed in a camouflaged bush jacket, green* US *Army
> Special Forces tee-shirt and a baseball cap. He carries a Colt* AR – 15
> *automatic rifle. He glances at the lightbulb and turns in the doorway.*

HECK (*shouts off-stage*). Chicano! Start the generator!

> HECK *removes his bush jacket and hangs it carefully on a nail.*

> CASCABEL's *legs appear in the window and he jumps off the roof
> onto the balcony. The antennae wires dangle across the window.*

HECK. Burn the school?

   PEDRO *nods.*

HECK. Lost your tongue?

PEDRO. No.

HECK. What happened to Delta Patrol?

   PEDRO *shrugs.*

HECK. When did you arrive?

PEDRO. Hour ago.

HECK. Any sign they'd bin and gone?

PEDRO. Who?

HECK. Delta!

PEDRO. No.

   CASCABEL *sits outside the window on the balcony. His head can be seen, as he bends over the radio.*

   HECK *speaks through the window to him.*

HECK. That thing work?

CASCABEL. Yup.

HECK. Phone Delta and ask him where he is and what happened to our rendezvous. Tell him we're leaving this ant heap tomorrow at dawn with or without him.

   CASCABEL *places the headset on his head and speaks.*

CASCABEL (*into the mike*). Sierra Seven, Sierra Seven, this is Sierra Five, d'you read me Sierra Seven, . . .

HECK. These the prisoners?

PEDRO. Yes.

HECK. All y'get? Three?

PEDRO. Yes.

   Enter JULIO

HECK (*to* JULIO). Where were you?

JULIO. With Pedro.

HECK (*to* PEDRO). He with you?

PEDRO. Yes.

HECK (*to* JULIO). Any sign of Delta?

JULIO. No.

HECK. I wanna wash.

   JULIO *starts to go out.*

HECK. Julio –

JULIO. Yeah?

HECK. Done a count?

JULIO. No.

HECK. Do a count.

   Exit JULIO.

HECK (*to* LOUISA). Name? . . . What's your name?

LOUISA. I've asked for some water.

HECK. Tell me your name.

LOUISA. Tell me yours.

HECK. My name is Henry Ma'am but my buddies call me
   Heck. I like to think they call me Heck for bein' a heck of a
   guy but I know they call me Heck 'cus I'm Henry. I fall over
   myself to live up to my name.

   A loud burst of automatic gunfire, off-stage, propels HECK *to the
   doorway.*

HECK (*yells, off-stage*). Hey! Sanchez! Son of a bitch cut that
   out! . . . Hey! Sanchez! C'min here!

   HECK *yawns and rubs his face. He opens a bottle of Ron Plata and
   takes a long pull.*

   Enter SANCHEZ, *a cocky young Contra aged 18. He goes to the case
   of rum and takes a bottle out.*

HECK. What happened?

SANCHEZ. When?

HECK. Back in Jalapa. You were supposed to give me covering
   fire.

SANCHEZ. We did.

HECK. That cotton's knee high Sanchez –

SANCHEZ. We lost three men.

HECK. How the hell am I supposed to know that? I almost had my head blown off . . .

SANCHEZ. Didn't though did ya.

HECK. I'm not here to take risks Sanchez. You guys get your heads blown off, I'm the adviser. My head stays put.

Enter JULIO *with some water.* HECK *starts to wash.* JULIO *searches for chocolate.*

Enter ECO. *He finds a brand new tee-shirt, wrapped in polythene and removes his own which is covered in blood. He exits with the new tee-shirt.*

SANCHEZ *shows* EMILIO *a photo of the Pope.*

SANCHEZ. Know who that is?

EMILIO. Pope.

SANCHEZ. He's on our side.

SANCHEZ *rummages amongst the tarpaulins.*

HECK. You had flame-thrower instruction?

SANCHEZ. No but I know how to use 'em.

HECK. No you don't. Not if you haven't had instruction.

SANCHEZ *inspects a hammock.*

Exit JULIO *with chocolate.*

HECK (*to* PEDRO). Interrogate 'em?

PEDRO. I waited for you.

HECK. I can't do it Pedro, I'm the advisor.

SANCHEZ. I'll do it.

HECK. Had instruction?

SANCHEZ. I read the manual.

HECK. You can't read! (*Pause.*) So goddam humid up here.

HECK *finds four water canteens and exits.*

Enter JULIO, *eating chocolate.*

PEDRO. Do a count?

JULIO. Yup.

PEDRO. Any missing?

JULIO. Three.

PEDRO. Who?

JULIO. Fausto, Gregorio and Santos.

JULIO hunts for more chocolate.

EMILIO (*to* SANCHEZ). You got Bugs Bunny in your camp?

SANCHEZ. Yup.

EMILIO. Tom and Jerry?

SANCHEZ. Yup.

EMILIO. Michael Jackson?

SANCHEZ. Yup.

EMILIO. Elmer Phudd?

SANCHEZ. Uh?

Exit SANCHEZ.

CASCABEL has picked up a signal on the radio.

CASCABEL. Sierra Five, I read you, very faint, say again, over –

Exit JULIO, eating more chocolate.

PEDRO (*to* LOUISA). Be careful how you speak to the Gringo –

CASCABEL. – come in Sierra Five . . . say again, over –

PEDRO. – he's a shithead.

Enter HECK. He carries four canteens full of water. He keeps one for himself and hands the other three to the prisoners.

The prisoners drink.

Enter JOSUE limping with one boot off. He finds a first aid box and searches in that.

HECK *walks to the window.*

HECK. Raise Delta?

CASCABEL nods and gestures with his hand to say 'Wait'.

HECK. What's your name?

LOUISA. Louisa Riguerro.

HECK. Y'a Brigadista?

LOUISA. No.

HECK. Midwife?

LOUISA. No.

HECK. Teach school?

LOUISA. I am a schoolteacher.

HECK. How many schools in that place? Name of the town
  Pedro? Place we just shot up . . .

PEDRO. Jalapa.

HECK. Yeah. How many schools?

LOUISA. One.

  Exit JOSUE *with a tin of ointment and plasters.*

HECK. Goddam howler monkeys. You hear howler monkeys
  Pedro?

PEDRO. No.

HECK. Get 'em in Managua?

PEDRO. No.

  Enter CHICANO. *He searches for a shovel.*

HECK. Y'get howler monkeys in Jalapa Louisa? They disrupt
  class?

LOUISA. No.

PEDRO. They live in the mountains.

HECK. This ain't a mountain it's a hill. Name of this hill
  Pedro –

PEDRO. Chachagua Mountain.

HECK. It's a goddam hill! Hey. Chicano . . .

  CHICANO *exits, holding the ass of his trousers and waving the shovel
  in the air.*

HECK. Goddam butterflies. Drive me insane. What's your
  name kid?

EMILIO. Emilio.

CASCABEL (*through the window*). Delta's bin shot up.

HECK. How bad?

CASCABEL. There's three left.

HECK. Who?

CASCABEL. Didn't say.

HECK. Did you ask?

CASCABEL. They didn't hear me.

HECK. They ambushed?

CASCABEL. They walked into six truck-loads of Sandinista soldiers.

HECK. Six truck-loads?

CASCABEL. This morning on the road from Jalapa to Ocotal.

HECK. What in hell were they doin' there?

CASCABEL. Delta lost twenty-one men and the Sandinistas went on to Jalapa.

HECK *goes to the door.*

PEDRO. They'll be comin' after us.

HECK. Sanchez! (*To* PEDRO.) How much start do we have on 'em? Cascabel get me HQ, ask for Jackson – half a day?

PEDRO. At least.

HECK. I can't figure it out. Delta was ahead of us . . .

HECK *picks up a pile of M-60 ammo belts.*

Enter SANCHEZ.

HECK. I want our six best men on the ridge up there.

HECK *hands the ammo belts to* SANCHEZ.

SANCHEZ. What?

HECK. And break camp. We head off in two hours.

SANCHEZ. We only just got here.

HECK. There's a horde of Sandinistas on our tail.

SANCHEZ. We can fight 'em

HECK. Six truck-loads asshole. That's a battalion.

CASCABEL. Got Jackson.

HECK *goes to the window.*

HECK (*to* SANCHEZ). Post the men and come back here.

Exit SANCHEZ.

HECK *takes the headset.*

HECK. Tex? It's Alpha . . . we're stuck on this pile of ratshit they call a mountain . . . name of the place Pedro –

PEDRO. You don't say it over the –

HECK. – Chachagua that's it . . . Tex . . . you with me? . . . we got three hundred Sandinistas heading this way . . . what's your airborne?

PEDRO. You've given away our position.

Enter JULIO. *He picks up a tarpaulin, bottle of rum and more chocolate.*

HECK. Three hundred Sandinistas and our strength's thirty men . . . we can't hold this position Tex . . . if you could send us a chopper . . . you got no Huey's? All we need's one Huey load of men and some RPG's . . . they're half a day behind us . . . that's too late Tex . . . (*To* PEDRO.) How many days are we outa' Cifuentes?

PEDRO. Three.

HECK. Three days march from Cifuentes and a half a day from combat Tex it don't add up . . . you'd have to transport 'em through the air . . . I understand Tex . . . what?

Enter JOSUE. *He picks up a tarpaulin and two bottles of rum. He wears an M-60 ammo belt.*

PEDRO. Where you goin'?

JOSUE. Ridge.

PEDRO. Don't get drunk.

JOSUE. Why?

Exit JOSUE.

HECK. . . . oh, right, I got you . . . I'm with you Tex . . . (*He checks his watch, a gold Rolex.*) We'll stick around here till the heat's gone. We'll strike off at 3pm Tex. That'll give us three hours today . . . have a fleet of Toyotas waiting at Cifuentes

with their engines running midday Wednesday Tex . . . roger
. . . sure . . . and a round of golf . . .

He hands the headset back to CASCABEL.

PEDRO. That was a crazy thing to do . . .

HECK. Can you believe that? All I ask is one lousy Huey 500
and we could win this fuckin' war!

HECK stands in the doorway.

HECK. Eco! Cancer! Chicano! Where's Coyote?

SANCHEZ enters.

SANCHEZ. He took an M-60 up on the ridge.

PEDRO. There's no Hueys.

SANCHEZ. I can fly a Huey.

CONTRAS have gathered outside.

HECK stands in the doorway.

HECK (*to* SANCHEZ). Delta's wiped out and the dogs of hell
are on our tail. We march at three. Tell the men to clean their
weapons and count out rounds. Sixteen hundred each. (*Yells,
off-stage.*) Chico. Eco. Come in here and take a box of ammo
out.

Enter CHICO *and* ECO. *They take a box of ammo each and exit.*

HECK. Cascabel. On the roof. Julio!

CASCABEL climbs up on the roof.

HECK. Grenades –

SANCHEZ passes a box of grenades over to HECK *who passes them
up through the window to* CASCABEL *on the roof.*

Enter JULIO, *eating chocolate.*

HECK. Emilio. Empty your pockets.

EMILIO starts to empty his pockets onto a crate.

HECK finds a tin of pineapple chunks and slings it across to JULIO.

Enter CHICO *and* ECO. *They carry open ammo boxes.*

CHICO. These are the wrong cartridges.

HECK. Uh?

SANCHEZ inspects the cartridges.

ECO. They're SLRs.

HECK. What are your weapons?

SANCHEZ. M1s.

HECK. SLR fit an M1?

SANCHEZ. 'course not.

HECK. There's bound to be a boxa M1 cartridges here someplace . . .

CHICO *and* ECO *hunt for M1 cartridge boxes. During the following interrogations they turn the place upside down with a building urgency and vigour.*

HECK. Hey! Where in hell d'ya get this? How old are ya?

EMILIO. Fifteen.

HECK *holds up a handful of dollars which* EMILIO *has taken from his pocket.*

HECK. You are one rich kid! Where d'you earn this?

EMILIO. Managua.

HECK. Managua? That's a hell of a way from home. What're you doin' in Managua kid?

EMILIO. Shinin' shoes.

HECK. Shoeshine! Sanchez we have an entrepreneur in our midst! A go-getter! Good boy! Good kid! Good fella!

JULIO *has opened the pineapple and hands it to* HECK. HECK *eats pineapple from the tin.*

PEDRO *goes to the window and calls out.*

PEDRO. Snake!

HECK. What d'you want?

PEDRO. I want Cascabel.

HECK. Why?

CASCABEL*'s head appears at the top of the window.*

CASCABEL. Yeah?

PEDRO (*to* HECK). I want to ask him something.

HECK. What?

PEDRO. I want to ask him if he could swear it was Delta Patrol he spoke with on the radio.

HECK. Who the fuck else was it Cowboy?

CASCABEL. No.

PEDRO. You couldn't be sure.

CASCABEL. No.

HECK. Who else knows the frequency? Who else knows the call sign? We coulda bin anybody . . .

CASCABEL's *face disappears from the window.*

PEDRO. If they had Delta's radio . . .

HECK. Delta had Delta's radio.

PEDRO *reads his bible.*

HECK. You. Name.

ALDO. My name is Aldo Munoz.

HECK. How old are you?

ALDO. I am forty.

HECK. What are ya, Campesino?

ALDO. Yes.

HECK. What's the matter Aldo?

ALDO. Nothing.

HECK. You're shivering. You cold?

ALDO. No.

HECK. Afraid?

ALDO. Naturally.

HECK. Why? We're all Campesinos here. I'm not. I'm the advisor but Pedro, he's a Campesino. You a Campesino Pedro?

PEDRO. Yes.

HECK. Sanchez?

SANCHEZ. What?

HECK. You a Campesino?

SANCHEZ. Yeah.

HECK. See? You're in good company. You a zonal co-ordinator or any shit like that?

ALDO. I'm not a zonal co-ordinator.

HECK. You on the Sandinista Defence Committee?

ALDO. Yes.

HECK. Hear that? He's CDS.

PEDRO. They all are.

HECK. You farm on your own?

ALDO. I am a member of a co-operative.

HECK. What kinda co-operative?

ALDO. We grow cotton.

HECK. I know that.

ALDO. We are a production co-operative.

HECK. That the one where no one owns the land?

ALDO. We all own the land.

HECK. Who forced that one on ya, Castro?

ALDO. No he did not.

HECK. Ortega?

ALDO. We debated it and took a vote.

HECK. My ass.

ALDO. That's the truth.

HECK. Who runs this co-operative?

ALDO. We have a President, three secretaries of production, finance and education, and representatives who sit on the committee.

HECK. D'you sit on this committee?

ALDO. I do.

HECK. Who d'you have to buy to get onto this committee?

ALDO. I was nominated and subsequently elected.

HECK. By whom?

ALDO. By the members of the co-operative.

HECK. Who nominated you?

ALDO. Who nominated me?

HECK. I'm askin' you who it was nominated you.

ALDO. A man named Umberto.

HECK. He on the committee?

ALDO. No he is not.

HECK. He the President? Those fuckin' Hondurans, they're for ever playin' golf . . .

ALDO. He holds no elected position.

HECK. Who?

ALDO. Umberto.

HECK. Why not?

ALDO. He has chosen not to.

HECK. Was he nominated?

ALDO. I don't remember.

HECK. You don't remember? And you call yourself a democracy?

LOUISA. He was nominated.

HECK. I'm not askin' you!

ALDO. It has nothing to do with democracy whether you can remember if somebody was nominated or not.

HECK. I say it has everything to do with democracy. I reckon this Umberto's a persecuted man . . .

ALDO. No, I'm sorry you're wrong . . .

HECK. I say his case should be taken before the Court of Human Rights.

LOUISA. Umberto was nominated for Production Secretary but he turned it down because he didn't wish to serve. That's his right.

HECK. Who nominated Umberto?

PEDRO. This is crazy . . .

LOUISA. I nominated Umberto ...

HECK. You teach school.

LOUISA. Yes.

HECK. You his woman?

LOUISA. Umberto's? Certainly not.

HECK. How come you get to nominate people onto the council?

LOUISA. Of course I can nominate ...

HECK. Can women nominate?

PEDRO. 'course they can.

HECK. You're a member of the co-operative?

LOUISA. Yes.

HECK. (*to* ALDO). She a member?

ALDO. Yes she is a member.

HECK. You teach school. You don't own land.

ALDO. None of us own the land. We all own it.

HECK. But she teaches school.

LOUISA. Somebody has to teach in the school and others work on the land.

HECK. Does Umberto work on the land?

ALDO. Yes. Umberto works on the land.

HECK. He happy with that?

ALDO. Of course.

HECK. What function does Umberto serve on the committee?

LOUISA. We've told you. He doesn't have a function.

HECK. I'd say a man without a function is a man without hope wouldn't you Pedro? A man without dignity. A man without freedom. What is your function Comrade?

ALDO. Mine?

HECK. Yes.

ALDO. What do you mean by function?

HECK. On the committee.

ALDO. My function on the committee.

HECK. It's what I asked.

ALDO. I am the Pesticides Representative.

HECK. The Pesticides Representative! Well bust my buttons where can he go from here?

ALDO. I wish to go home. You have no right to keep us here. You have no grounds to hold us against our will.

HECK *takes a roll of bills from his bush jacket pocket.*

HECK. Sanchez. For five hundred bucks . . .

CHICO *has finished hunting for cartridges.*

CHICO. There's no M1s, it's all SLRs.

HECK. There's a boxa M1s here Chico you just haven't looked!

PEDRO. We distributed that box before the offensive . . .

HECK. All of 'em?

PEDRO. There was only thirty thousand in the box.

HECK. Where d'ya think these things come from Pedro, grow on trees?

CHICO. We gotta dozen rounds between us.

HECK *is counting out five hundred dollars.*

PEDRO. It's serious. We have no ammunition for our weapons.

SANCHEZ. We got three M-60s.

CHICO. They're on the ridge.

PEDRO. Bring 'em down.

HECK. Leave 'em there.

SANCHEZ. Bring down Coyote.

HECK. They're most effective on the ridge.

PEDRO *is at the door.*

PEDRO. Chicano!

CHICO (*indicates* HECK). He carrying an SLR?

PEDRO. 'course 'e is. Every fuckin' commando in this unit's issued with an M1 and the Gringo picks an SLR.

CHICANO *has arrived.*

PEDRO. Go up on the ridge and bring down two M-60s.

HECK. You stay put Chicano ...

PEDRO. Don't listen to him. He's just the advisor ...

HECK. That's right! I'm the advisor! I'm not the asshole in the
armour pool who issues SLR bullets to a unit armed with M1s!

PEDRO. You're lucky to have an SLR. You have ammunition.
We don't.

HECK. Here. Take the SLR. Godammit take it. Gimme your M1!

They exchange weapons.

HECK. And here's a box of SLRs.

HECK *kicks a box of cartridges over to* PEDRO, *who loads the SLR
and fills his pouches with cartridges.*

PEDRO. Now we should go.

HECK. We go when I say.

PEDRO. We can't risk a confrontation.

HECK. There won't be one.

PEDRO. Don't trust the radio. We don't know where the
Sandinistas are. They could be here already.

HECK. Delta said ...

PEDRO. You can't be certain it was Delta ...

HECK. Sanchez ...

SANCHEZ. Yup?

HECK. For five hundred bucks ...

PEDRO. Come on ...

HECK. You got your goddam SLR! Now siddown! Read your
bible!

PEDRO *does as he's told.*

HECK. Take old Aldo here outside, strip him bare-assed naked
and tie him to a tree. That tree, the tree we can all see ...

PEDRO. The unit's in danger ...

HECK. Then you can carve the meat off his legs ...

SANCHEZ *has frogmarched* ALDO *to the door.*

SANCHEZ. Right.

HECK. You bin instructed how to do that?

SANCHEZ. We had lessons.

HECK. The bottom half of his legs.

SANCHEZ. Yup.

LOUISA. This is immoral . . .

HECK. Next you cut his balls off . . .

LOUISA. You can't do this . . .

SANCHEZ. Will do . . .

LOUISA (*to* PEDRO). Stop him . . .

HECK. After that you slit his throat and pull his tongue down through the slit. Get to that in boot camp?

SANCHEZ. Eco's done that.

LOUISA (*to* PEDRO). Can't you shoot him?

PEDRO. They've got M-60s out there. They're twice the size of these.

Exit SANCHEZ *with* ALDO

LOUISA. This is barbaric! You can't do it! For God's sake! What d'you think you're doing!

HECK *is standing in the doorway, looking out. Feet apart, hands in pockets, rocking on the balls of his feet.*

HECK. Oh Sanchez!

SANCHEZ (*off, at a distance*). What?

HECK. Most important of all! When you done that you take him down the hill and dump him on the highway! Some place nice and busy where the Sandinistas will find him.

SANCHEZ (*off*). Yeah!

HECK *finds a cassette player and plugs it into the light socket. He plays New York disco music, loud.*

Then he grabs EMILIO *by the hair and makes him watch through the window.*

Pause.

When ALDO'*s torture is over* HECK *releases* EMILIO.
He unplugs the cassette player.

HECK. You read?

EMILIO *can hardly speak.*

EMILIO (*mumbles*). Yes.

Enter ECO, *his hands covered in blood.*

HECK. Who took him down the hill?

ECO. Sanchez.

HECK. Sanchez. On his own?

ECO. Yes.

ECO *finds a canteen of water and washes the blood off his hands.*

HECK *counts two hundred dollars off his roll of bills as he talks to* EMILIO.

HECK. Wanna learn how to read real good?

LOUISA. He's a fluent reader.

HECK. Maybe get to high school?

EMILIO *can't speak.*

HECK. C'mon, you're a bright kid. You have initiative. You earn money and save it. You get your hands dirty shining shoes. You have a future, maybe get to Harvard. Play baseball?

EMILIO (*mumbles*). Yeah.

HECK. What are you, batter?

EMILIO (*mumbles*). Pitcher.

HECK. Popular game in this country isn't it?

EMILIO *nods.*

HECK *hands* ECO *two hundred dollars.* ECO *pockets it.*

HECK. You could get to fly a jet fighter, how about that?

EMILIO *shrugs.*

HECK. Make your Momma real proud. Gotta Momma?

EMILIO (*mumbles*). Yes.

HECK. Gotta Poppa?

EMILIO *shakes his head.*

HECK. What happened to your father, son?

EMILIO (*mumbles*). Dead.

HECK. Dead? I'm truly sorry to hear that Emilio. Truly sorry. How did he die?

EMILIO (*mumbles*). You just killed 'im.

HECK. Pardon me?

EMILIO (*louder*). You just killed 'im.

HECK. Me? I never killed anyone. I'm the advisor.

HECK *rounds on* LOUISA.

HECK. Stand up!

LOUISA. No!

HECK (*indicates the bedroom*). Get in there.

LOUISA. No.

HECK. Go on!

LOUISA. You won't lay a hand on me! You won't touch me! You bastard! You shithead!

HECK (*to* ECO). Get her in there.

ECO *manhandles* LOUISA *into the bedroom. She screams and fights all the way.*

HECK *removes his boots and starts to undress.*

HECK. Pedro as I'm the guy who's bin doin' all the work around here I figure I'm first on board. Then Eco here, he earned second place then Sanchez three, Cascabel's four, Chicano, Chico, Pedro I don't put you any more than eight or ten down the line. Can you argue with that?

PEDRO. Those men out there have no ammunition.

HECK. Unless you can think of anything you can do to redeem your position, maybe claw your way back to one ahead of Coyote?

PEDRO. I'm not bothered.

HECK. Whassamadder, y'a fruit?

HECK's *trousers are off.*

Inside the bedroom LOUISA *is struggling and screaming.* HECK *walks to the bedroom.*

HECK. Take her dress off.

LOUISA. No!

The sound of LOUISA *being struck.*

PEDRO *chambers a round in his SLR.* EMILIO *slides towards the tarpaulins.*

There is the sound of gunfire, down the slope. Then there's the sound of heavier, M-60 fire from closer to hand and all hell breaks loose outside.

Gunfire and screams of injured and dying men.

PEDRO *runs to the door.*

PEDRO (*shouts*). Come back here! Reform you fucking rabbits!

He goes to the bedroom door.

PEDRO. Come on! Come on!

LOUISA *comes out of the bedroom.* PEDRO *grabs her and runs to the doorway.*

PEDRO. Where's the kid?

LOUISA. Emilio! Emilio!

EMILIO *is nowhere to be seen.*

PEDRO. Come on! (*Exit* PEDRO *and* LOUISA.)

HECK *rushes from the bedroom. He looks for his trousers.*

More gunfire. Closer to hand. HECK *scuttles back into the bedroom.*

CASCABEL *falls on the roof.*

The antennae and grenades slide down the roof and onto the veranda.

Then CASCABEL's *face appears upside down dripping blood at the top of the window frame. Dead.*

Silence.

The tarpaulins move. EMILIO *emerges from underneath the tarpaulins.*

Nearby, a monkey howls. EMILIO *turns and sees* CASCABEL's *face. He opens the door and cautiously steps out onto the balcony. A burst of automatic gunfire sends him scuttling back indoors. Bullets hail on the zinc roof.*

CASCABEL's *body is dislodged and it slides down onto the veranda.*

Silence.

Nearby a monkey howls. A single shot rings out and silences the monkey.

EMILIO *is crouched against the wall.*

HECK *emerges from the bedroom. He walks across the hut and picks up his trousers. Ignoring* EMILIO, HECK *returns to the bedroom carrying his trousers.*

HECK *is framed in the bedroom doorway when the door to the hut bursts open and* SANCHEZ *enters.*

SANCHEZ. Freeze, jack.

HECK *stands in the doorway to the bedroom, his back to* SANCHEZ *and his hands in the air.*

SANCHEZ *carries a Kalashnikov. He shoots* HECK *in the back.* HECK *falls forward into the bedroom, dead.*

SANCHEZ *opens a bottle of rum and drinks.*

SANCHEZ. Show us your feet.

EMILIO *doesn't move.*

SANCHEZ *takes off one of* EMILIO*'s shoes. A battered trainer.*

SANCHEZ. Thass no good.

SANCHEZ *goes to the window and scans the outside.*

Thass the trouble when you're fighting your own people. You can never make out who the fuck you're talkin' to on the radio.

SANCHEZ *throws* EMILIO *the Kalashnikov.*

SANCHEZ. Load that.

Exit SANCHEZ.

EMILIO *is too shocked to move.*

After some time he edges towards the Kalashnikov and picks it up. A boot sails through the window and hits him square in the back. He drops the Kalashnikov.

Outside SANCHEZ *laughs.*

SANCHEZ (*from off-stage*). Try it on!

EMILIO *picks the boot up.*

SANCHEZ *sticks his head through the door.*

SANCHEZ. That's Chico's. You're about his size. I'll get you his fatigues.

Exit SANCHEZ.

EMILIO *picks up the Kalashnikov again.*

SANCHEZ *enters with a tiger suit and another boot. He throws the suit over* EMILIO's *head.*

EMILIO *drops the Kalashnikov.*

SANCHEZ. Haven't you loaded it yet? Put this on. And the boot.

SANCHEZ *picks up* HECK's *trousers and takes out the remaining dollar bills. He pockets them.*

I don't like Gringos. I can't see why we have to have 'em. It was a Gringo issued us with SLR slugs insteada M1s.

EMILIO *hasn't touched the uniform.*

SANCHEZ. Put it on. It ain't gonna bite ya. You'll never last with that flimsy crap on where we're goin'.

During the following speech EMILIO *familiarises himself with* CHICO's *fatigues, strips and puts them on.* SANCHEZ *finds C-rations, a water canteen, poncho, tarpaulin and pup tent.*

You can fire an SLR from a Kalashnikov 'cos the Kalashnikov's Russian and the SLR's Israeli. They don't fit the M1 cos M1s are Belgian and the Belgians are at war with Russia. There's a war on in Europe, bin a war on there for years and the Israelis are with the Russians and Gaddafi, he's French, supplied the FDN, that's us, with the M1's. We used to get Colts when the Gringos were at peace with Congress but then North, he's President of Congress, declared war on the Gringos and the fuckin' Colts dried up. Colt's a Gringo gun and that's a rarity now, favoured by the Gringos 'cos they stick to their own. They won't go near the Hondurans. The Gringos needed their Colts to fight Congress then they beat Congress and Congress surrendered and President North was exiled with his wife who wore out her shoes and he and a fella called Hull who's gotta ranch in Costa Rica started flyin' drugs to the Ayatollah, hearda him? He's British. Fanatic. Fought the Argentines. In order to finance Congress, who wanted to re-arm and fight the Russians who supply the Sandinistas with their Kalashnikovs! See? So North had a fence in Miami, feller called Bush who's gotta ranch in Guatamala with an airstrip big enough to take the transport planes, so one day we started getting armoured cars, bearcats and RPGs and goddam Huey helicopters turnin' up at the camp from Bush who's floggin' cocaine to the Ayatollah in order to keep us in arms to fight the Sandinistas who are supplied by the Russians who're at war with Belgium who's the Ayatollah's ally! That's how we got the M1s! Gaddafi! And Bush!

Every Tuesday we attend a class on world affairs. In the camp. 'Cos you gotta keep abreast of what the hell's goin' on. 'Cos if you don't you dunno what you're fighting for. And if you dunno what you're fighting for you're dead. With me?

SANCHEZ *picks up the Kalashnikovs and carries them outside.*

EMILIO *stands in the middle of the hut, lost, half-dressed, one boot on.*

Enter SANCHEZ *wearing a bandana round his mouth.*

SANCHEZ. They've started stinkin' already. That ole geezer I took down the slope, he'll be half eaten by dogs by now.

SANCHEZ *dresses* EMILIO *whilst speaking.*

'E reminded me of my father that old fella. Same ole shit he was comin' out with about Defence Committees, president this electing that. I said to 'im I said Pop, is that what you want? Two little acres and a rooster? Is this all you want outa the Revolution? 'Cos it ain't enough for me Pop. Bloody technicos comin' up and tellin' 'im what to grow, where to grow, lemon trees here, coffee there, money for this, nothin' for that, join this organisation and help thy neighbour with that and all this for two fuckin' acres of scratch! And a rooster! And he was happy! He was like a pig in shit! Till they skinned 'im. I watched 'em do it. Yanked his skin off like a coat. They make you watch y'know. (*Taps his forehead.*) They did a lotta butcherin' that night, the Contras. Two guys did it all.

SANCHEZ *kits* EMILIO *out with rucksack, belt, canteen etc.*

SANCHEZ. They slashed my uncle's throat, I saw that as well. He was a good man. Better'n my Pop. The leader of the Contras at that time was Suicida. He skinned my dad. He's dead now. So's his S-2, Krill. Suicida killed Krill 'cos Krill was fuckin' Suicida's woman then Suicida's woman killed Suicida for killin' Krill. She's dead too. She was blown up in a truck at Cifuentes. We got three days hump through jungle before we hit a road. Hundred clicks. Know what a click is? Kilometre. Ten miles.

SANCHEZ *hands* EMILIO PEDRO'*s bible and exits.*

EMILIO *is dressed up like a Christmas tree. He stands in the middle of the room, opens the bible and stares blankly at the page.*

Enter SANCHEZ *with* CHICANO *over his shoulder. He throws* CHICANO *down. Then he unties* CHICANO'*s bandana from round his neck and ties it round* EMILIO'*s mouth.*

SANCHEZ. I've left Chico out there 'cos 'e's bollock naked and the dogs'll 'ave 'im.

He kits himself up.

There was no survivors besides us. Right? The Gringo died fighting. Hand to hand with a machete. There was three hundred Sandinistas. It was a special Mobile Unit. BLI. Crack troops.

SANCHEZ *finds a grenade. He leads* EMILIO *to the door.*

Right. I'm gonna blow this lot up. So you run to the edge of the clearing and lie down behind that tree we tied the old man to.

EMILIO *wanders off.*

SANCHEZ *goes out and shuts the door. He appears at the window. He removes the pin of the grenade.*

SANCHEZ. Alright?

SANCHEZ *carefully lobs the grenade into the centre of the room.*

He runs to the edge of the clearing. There is a bright flash of light and then:

Blackout.

Scene Two
KISSING THE POPE

·Honduras.
Three days later. Late afternoon. Fifteen kilometres inside the Honduran border. The top of a mountain.

Enter EMILIO. *He staggers under the weight of his haversack.*

SANCHEZ *(from off-stage).* Stop!

EMILIO *collapses. He is exhausted.*

Enter SANCHEZ. *He places the Kalashnikovs under a tree. He speaks as he unbuckles his harness and lowers his haversack.*

Always bivouac on top of a mountain. You're above the enemy and you gotta downhill start in the morning. (*Taps his forehead.*) Psychological see?

Exit SANCHEZ.

EMILIO *is on his back with his haversack beneath him. He is too tired to get up. He jerks himself over onto his side.*

Enter SANCHEZ *with two yucca roots.*

Eat yucca?

SANCHEZ *unhooks his water canteen from his belt and washes the yucca. He slings a yucca to* EMILIO *and starts chewing his. He looks around him, reconnoitring.*

Old cattle trail this. Can't light a fire yet. You think you're safe and they grow up out the ground in front of you, Sandinistas, like ghosts.

He manhandles EMILIO *onto his front and unstraps his rolled up groundsheet and poncho-liner.*

Leave mosta this behind tomorrer. Travel light the last day.

He hikes EMILIO *up onto his knees.*

EMILIO *unbuckles his harness, lets slip the haversack and collapses to the ground.*

SANCHEZ *unpacks his haversack. He unclips a torch from his uniform breast and places it close by. He takes an optimus stove from his haversack. Then he takes a tin of baked beans, two aluminium hash-cans, tin-opener, spoons and lighter. He opens the beans and starts cooking.*

He is speaking whilst unpacking.

SANCHEZ. We're moving into big-unit warfare now we've got the numbers. Upper echelon's planning an offensive on Ocotal in the very near future. We're putting three thousand men into Ocotal. Clear a landing strip and declare the town a liberated area. So the non-aligned countries like NATO can send us aid direct to Ocotal. From there we free the north-eastern sector, march south, and liberate Managua. After that we take a shower. Hah! (*He laughs.*)

Howler monkeys shriek.

Fulla Russians, Managua. Fulla Cubans. Know what they do? They piss in hypodermics and inject the babies with it. Then they bite the babies' heads off as they're dying. They cut off men's balls and fry 'em. Cubans go to war over a man's balls to eat. Castro eats 'em by the cart-load. Since he quit cigars Cuba's fulla eunuchs. The Sandinistas force their women to eat their own afterbirth to make 'em fecund. Disgusts me. The priests are forced to eat their own shit and all the churches used as brothels.

The beans are cooking. SANCHEZ *eats his yucca.* EMILIO *is too tired to eat.*

SANCHEZ. Come on. Eat your yucca.

EMILIO *takes a bite.*

SANCHEZ. Fuck knows what we're gonna find when we take Managua. The misery.

The beans are nearly ready. SANCHEZ *stirs them.*

They'll be mobilising when we get back, for Ocotal. But you and me won't be going. I'll make sure a that. 'Cos Ocotal's gonna be a bloodbath whoever wins. Thass why we gotta make fuckin' sure I get two stripes, a citation and my picture in the *Miami Herald.* So we get a special op' a long way from Ocotal. With me?

SANCHEZ *takes the pan off the stove and hands it to* EMILIO.

EMILIO *takes the beans.*

Hot enough for ya?

EMILIO *nods and starts to eat slowly.* SANCHEZ *starts to cook his beans.*

SANCHEZ. I'll have to dream up a nom de guerre for the *Miami Herald.*

He stirs his beans.

I take the Pope with me wherever I go 'cos I'm killin' for the Pope. Thass the first thing they tell you at Camp. You gotta have a reason and you gotta know why. Then they show you how. First thing you do is close-quarter combat with an Irish chap called El Chino. 'Cos to kill with one a them (*Indicates Kalashnikov.*) is nothin'. But to kill at arm's length requires the deftness of a surgeon and the ferocity of a rabid dog.

He starts to eat. He indicates the stove.

I'm keepin' that on for a special reason. El Chino says kill without joy. 'Cos the first time you do it it's like sex, you wanna do it, you have to, but you're nervous. Your hands are sweatin'. Your knees are knockin'.

He stands and puts his beans down.

And I used to do this, 'cos your lung collapses onto your stomach that's what makes you sick. Y'ad sex? You gotta put your hands underneath your ribcage, bend down, deep breath, straighten up, gun out and shoot the bastard in the back or cock out dependin' on whether it's sex. You gotta remember which it is.

EMILIO *has stopped eating.* SANCHEZ *picks up the pans, the empty baked bean tins, the opener and the spoons, and goes away.*

EMILIO *stands.*

SANCHEZ *comes back.*

SANCHEZ. Won't be needing them again. I chucked 'em in the bushes way down, keep 'em outa sight of the beggar dogs. Bastards. Things they do. To the babies. Thass my reason. You'll have your own reason.

SANCHEZ *lays out the beds.*

Take your boots off and air your feet then put 'em back on again.

EMILIO *does as he's told.*

SANCHEZ. Not near me. Over there.

EMILIO *moves away and takes his boots off.*

SANCHEZ. Next geezer you see after El Chino is Icaza. In the Psychological Warfare Unit. So you've killed a man if you're lucky and you're knockin' on Icaza's door. Come in – he'll give you a personal welfare session. And if he likes you he'll give you more. He's a good man.

EMILIO *has his boots off. Some distance away.*

SANCHEZ. What was the name of that chap? You said? Back at Chachagua? There was Bugs Bunny, Tom and Jerry, Michael Jackson and who was the other one?

EMILIO. Elmer Phudd.

SANCHEZ. El Phudd.

SANCHEZ *takes a huge cigar from his haversack, lights it with the stove and extinguishes the flame. He slings the stove off, into the bushes.*

SANCHEZ. El Phudd. Yeah. I like it. (*He starts to remove his boots.*) I can command a unit. I can do anything. El Phudd. If you wanna kill me, kill me with my boots off. Whass yours, on or off?

EMILIO. Off.

SANCHEZ. Put 'em on.

EMILIO *puts his boots on.*

SANCHEZ. El Phudd. I like it.

SANCHEZ *lies on his bed and rests his head on his haversack. He smokes the cigar and drinks coke.*

SANCHEZ. He's like a father figure, old Icaza. 'Cos there's a lotta kids there without a father. And Icaza's like a father. You gotta father?

EMILIO. No.

SANCHEZ. Dead?

EMILIO. Yeah.

SANCHEZ. How did 'e die?

EMILIO. You killed 'im.

SANCHEZ *is silent. He smokes the cigar. Night has fallen. The torch is near* SANCHEZ.

Cicadas rattle. Bullfrogs croak. Monkeys shriek.

At length SANCHEZ *speaks.*

SANCHEZ. Play baseball?

EMILIO. Yeah.

SANCHEZ. Pitch or bat?

EMILIO. Pitcher.

SANCHEZ. Curveball or slider?

EMILIO. Both.

SANCHEZ. My ass.

EMILIO. Do.

SANCHEZ. I'm a spray-hitter.

EMILIO. They got teams in the camp?

SANCHEZ. 'course they have.

EMILIO. You on a team?

SANCHEZ. Yup.

EMILIO. Good one?

SANCHEZ. Not bad. I'm a fuckin' useful player thass why.

SANCHEZ *takes out his picture of the Pope.*

SANCHEZ. Wanna kiss the Pope?

SANCHEZ *kisses the Pope and passes it over to* EMILIO. *He then takes a rosary from his pocket and silently counts the beads.*

SANCHEZ. First thing they give you in the camp's a rosary, crucifix and a picture of the Pope. That's even before you see El Chino. Turn it over.

EMILIO *turns the Pope over.*

SANCHEZ. Put your hand over the torch and switch it on. Filter the light through your fingers.

EMILIO *does as he's told.*

Now read whass on the back.

EMILIO (*reads*). The Pope is with us. Christ is our liberator. With God and patriotism we will defeat Communism.

SANCHEZ *is praying silently with the rosary.*

SANCHEZ. Again?

EMILIO. The Pope is with us. Christ is our liberator. With God and Patriotism we will defeat Communism.

SANCHEZ. And again.

EMILIO. The Pope is with us. Christ is our liberator. With God and Patriotism we will defeat Communism.

SANCHEZ. Once more.

EMILIO. The Pope is with us. Christ is our liberator. With God and Patriotism we will defeat Communism.

EMILIO *falls asleep.*

SANCHEZ *takes the Pope and the torch from him. He checks his automatic's nearby, lies down and smokes his cigar.*

Pause.

He places his cigar beside his automatic and goes to sleep.

Bullfrogs croak. Cicadas rattle. Monkeys shriek.

Scene Three
AMERICAN DREAM

Honduras
Three weeks later. Night. The Military Instruction Camp at Danli.

A hut with two mattresses, two chairs, a window and a door. On the wall, a poster of the Pope.

> *Enter* SANCHEZ, *wearing fatigues. His bush jacket has two stripes on the arm and a large gold medal pinned on the chest. He carries bags of new clothes, a stetson, a ghetto blaster, a bottle of rum and a copy of the* Miami Herald. *He places all his baggage on the floor, and starts to drink rum.*

> *He opens the* Miami Herald *and finds a particular page, then places the paper, open at the page, onto the floor in a strategic position.*

> *He drinks.*

> *He removes his jacket and places it over the back of the chair making the stripes and gong visible. He then places the chair in a central position.*

> *He strips to his undershorts and dresses in his new clothes: a frilled shirt, open to the waist with the sleeves half rolled up; a medallion round his neck; drainpipe hipster jeans with a wide belt and turnups; cowboy boots, and a stetson.*

> *He smokes a cigar and drinks rum. He finds a tape and inserts it into the ghetto-blaster.*

> *Enter* EMILIO. *He wears baseball gear.*

> SANCHEZ *leaps from his seat.*

SANCHEZ. Kiss the Pope.

EMILIO. Why?

SANCHEZ. Kiss 'im!

> EMILIO *carries a Kingsize beefburger in one hand and a bottle of Coca Cola in the other. He walks to the wall and kisses the Pope.*

> SANCHEZ *indicates the newspaper on the floor.*

SANCHEZ. Read that.

EMILIO. What.

SANCHEZ. Miami Herald.

EMILIO *takes a bite from his burger.*

SANCHEZ. See the picture?

EMILIO. Yes?

SANCHEZ. Who it is?

EMILIO. Who?

SANCHEZ. Me!

Whilst SANCHEZ points out the photograph, EMILIO places his coke on the floor and his beefburger on the bed.

SANCHEZ. Look. That's me. Know who that is?

EMILIO. No.

SANCHEZ. That's Adolfo Calero! Read it. What it says. Underneath.

SANCHEZ sits on the bed. He sits on EMILIO's burger but doesn't notice.

EMILIO (*reads*). Tegucigalpa, Honduras, Monday . . . Tegucigalpa?

SANCHEZ. Read!

EMILIO (*reads*). Freedom Fighter El Phudd received the Presidential Medal for Bravery from FDN President Adolfo Calero Monday in the Rotunda Bar of the Honduran Maya Hotel . . . you were here Monday, in the camp . . .

SANCHEZ. That all there is?

EMILIO. No. There's more.

SANCHEZ. Read it!

EMILIO (*reads*). El Phudd was honoured for his heroic stand at the siege of Arenales in which he fought single-handedly against a battalion of the crack Sandinista BLI Regiment. The confrontation took place two weeks ago at the foot of Chachagua Mountain below the forward Contra base of Arenales. The Sandinistas were laying siege to a combat unit of the FDN. Fighting was fierce with crippling losses to the Sandinistas. In his citation President Calero said it was an immense tactical victory for the Democrats, calling El Phudd's action an outstanding example of individual bravery in the long struggle against Communism.

SANCHEZ. Christ! . . . Read it again.

EMILIO. All of it?

SANCHEZ. Citation. That bit . . .

EMILIO (*reads*). . . . in his citation President Calero said it was an immense tactical victory . . .

SANCHEZ. Yes?

EMILIO (*reads*). . . . calling El Phudd's action an outstanding example . . .

SANCHEZ. Hear that? Outstanding example!

EMILIO. Of individual bravery . . .

SANCHEZ. Individual bravery . . . that what it said?

EMILIO. . . . in the long struggle against Communism.

SANCHEZ. That it?

EMILIO. Yes.

EMILIO *shuts the paper and folds it. He hands it back to* SANCHEZ.

SANCHEZ *opens the paper and gazes at the photograph.*

EMILIO *looks round for his burger.*

SANCHEZ *passs* EMILIO *the rum.*

SANCHEZ. We're celebratin' tonight.

EMILIO *drinks.*

SANCHEZ. They've given me a patrol.

EMILIO. Oh.

SANCHEZ. Special Operations. So. Have a drink. 'Cos we're gonna celebrate.

EMILIO *drinks and looks for his burger.*

SANCHEZ. My S-1 said El Phudd. You are a sargent and a hero. Take command.

EMILIO. Good.

SANCHEZ. Pick a patrol 'e said. Four men. Four of the best. Any you like. From the whole camp. I knew who I wanted. Quick as a dash I rattled off a list of my loyal buddies and my S-1 said El Phudd! Take 'em! They're all yours! I said thank you sir. Much obliged. Is it Ocotal?

EMILO. Eh?

SANCHEZ. No 'e said. You're not goin' near Ocotal. I have a mission for you. Special mission. I kissed the Pope and thanked the blessed Virgin for gettin' me out of Ocotal so you gonna kiss the Pope?

EMILIO. I kissed the Pope.

SANCHEZ. Kiss 'im again.

EMILIO. You eat my burger?

SANCHEZ. Kiss the Pope!

EMILIO. Why?

SANCHEZ. Kiss 'im and I'll tell ya!

EMILIO *kisses the Pope.*

SANCHEZ. You were on my list.

EMILIO. What list?

SANCHEZ. You bin listening to me?

EMILIO. I had a burger when I came in 'ere.

It dawns on EMILIO *where his burger is.*

SANCHEZ. I told you I'd get us out of Ocotal and I've got us out of Ocotal. You and me ain't comin' back from Ocotal because we ain't goin'. And I tell ya summin else. The poor bastards who're goin' to Ocotal won't be comin' back, but I got us out of Ocotal so you gonna thank me?

EMILIO. Thank you.

SANCHEZ. So we got summin to celebrate. Tonight. You and me. On our own. 'Cos this hut's ours tonight.

EMILIO. Is it?

SANCHEZ. I've cleared it for sex.

EMILIO *is horrified.*

SANCHEZ. I've got two girls comin'. Fat one and a thin one. Which d'you like, fat or thin? Fat one's got big tits thin one's got no tits at all. Forget their names. I figured to meself if he want the fat one I'll have the thin one if he want the thin one I'll have the fat one 'cos I arn't fussed either way but some people's choosy, some like fat girls some like thin ones so if I get one of each he can have first choice so which d'you want, fat or thin? Fat one's got big tits thin one's got no tits at all. Fat one's gotta big ass whass the thin one's like? Thin I think. Fat one's big. Very big. Which d'ya want? Thin one?

EMILIO. Fat one.

SANCHEZ. You don't want the fat one! She's too big! Thin one isn' that thin! She gotta coupla tits! You have the thin one see how you get on and if you don't like the thin one we'll swap.

EMILIO. I want the fat one.

SANCHEZ. You can't have the fat one! I want the fat one!

EMILIO. You said you didn't mind!

SANCHEZ. Well I bin thinkin' I do mind and I want the fat one.

EMILIO. Then I'll have none at all.

SANCHEZ. What the hell's the thin one gonna do? Sit and watch?

EMILIO. Tell 'er not to come.

SANCHEZ. They're on their way!

EMILIO. When she gets here send her home again.

SANCHEZ. Don't you want sex?

EMILIO. Yes. With the fat one.

SANCHEZ. You can't have it with the fat one. No one ever wants the fat one. You're the first person I ever met who wants the fat one! Well I'll pull rank on this 'cos I got the stripes so I get the fat one.

EMILIO. You're sitting on my burger.

SANCHEZ. What?

EMILIO. You've sat on my burger.

SANCHEZ *stands*. EMILIO*'s burger is ingrained in the seat of his jeans.*

SANCHEZ. These jeans cost me forty dollars.

EMILIO. I'm sorry.

SANCHEZ. What the fuck am I supposed to do?

EMILIO. I'm . . .

SANCHEZ. I got two girls comin' . . .

EMILIO *is at the door.*

SANCHEZ. Where you goin'?

EMILIO. Get another burger. I'm starvin'.

SANCHEZ. Stay here!

SANCHEZ *reaches the door and shoves* EMILIO *out of the way. He opens the door, looks up and down and whistles. He hunts in his jacket and takes out a huge roll of bills.*

A CONTRA *comes to the door.*

SANCHEZ. Ten bucks any good to ya?

CONTRA. Yup.

SANCHEZ. Go to the fast food emporium and buy two Kingsize burgers. Fast.

The CONTRA *stays put.*

SANCHEZ. Now what?

CONTRA. Ten dollars.

SANCHEZ. You get your ten dollars when I get the burgers.

Exit CONTRA.

SANCHEZ *shuts the door.*

SANCHEZ (*indicates squashed burger*). Clear that up.

EMILIO *starts to clear up.* SANCHEZ *polishes his medal.*

SANCHEZ. Where you bin? With El Chino?

EMILIO. No.

SANCHEZ. Icaza.

EMILIO. Yes.

SANCHEZ. Personal Welfare Session.

EMILIO. Yes.

SANCHEZ. We should drink to our achievements. (*He indicates his medal.*) The gong.

EMILIO. The gong.

They drink.

SANCHEZ. The stripes.

EMILIO. The stripes.

They drink.

SANCHEZ. The citation.

EMILIO. The citation.

They drink.

SANCHEZ. The Miami Herald.

EMILIO. The Miami Herald.

They drink.

SANCHEZ. The bounty money.

EMILIO. What?

SANCHEZ. Money I got for you. Eight hundred bucks.

SANCHEZ *drinks.*

SANCHEZ. And getting out of Ocotal.

EMILIO. Getting out of Ocotal.

SANCHEZ. That's one helluva lot to celebrate.

SANCHEZ *drinks.*

SANCHEZ. I think you're right I should 'ave the fat one. Maria. I've had 'er before and she ah, she's very good with me. So if you've never done it you can watch.

A loud knock on the door.

SANCHEZ *panics.*

SANCHEZ. Christ! Me trousers! (*He searches for paper.*) Hold on! Wait! Don't come in! (*To* EMILIO.) Keep the door shut.

EMILIO *leans against the door.*

SANCHEZ *wipes his trousers with the paper* EMILIO *used to scrape the squashed burger off the bed.*

Another loud knock.

SANCHEZ. Wait!

SANCHEZ *bends over in front of* EMILIO, *who wipes the burger off his jeans. He then runs to the ghetto-blaster and presses the button.*

'Ramrod' by Bruce Springsteen plays. He shoves the stetson on his head – the price tag hangs down the back.

Finally he drapes himself on the bed.

SANCHEZ. How do I look?

EMILIO (*mumbles*). Bloody ridiculous.

SANCHEZ. Open the door.

EMILIO *opens the door. There's nobody there. Two Kingsize burgers sit on the ground outside the door.*

SANCHEZ. Ground!

He switches off the tape.

EMILIO *picks up the burgers and brings them inside.*

He shuts the door with his foot and offers a burger to SANCHEZ.

SANCHEZ. No.

EMILIO. Eh?

SANCHEZ. They're for you.

EMILIO. Uh?

SANCHEZ. That's a gift. From me.

EMILIO. Thanks.

EMILIO *stands with the beefburgers in his hands.*

SANCHEZ. Eat them.

EMILIO *sits in a chair holding a beefburger in each hand. He is too scared to put one down. He starts to eat.*

SANCHEZ *watches.*

SANCHEZ. There's men out there would shit on me if I let 'em. Hard to credit but it's true. They would see my stripes and gong and picture in the Miami Herald as a challenge for them to shit on me. They would roll a dice and invite me to join 'em. They'd smell my money like a dog can. They'd oil me up with rum and herd some girls in from the refugee sector on a bus. I'd decline the offer of sex and they would badger me, these curs, and sneer at my disinterest. They'd goad me and draw a crowd. Look at him they'd say. The decorated man. The hero. He don't have the stomach for dice or cards or whatever device they use for scavenging dollars off a loaded fool. And the rum'd push 'em further and they'd demonstrate their machismo by fornicating there and then before the other sodden louts. And before long one of these curs, I know which one . . .

EMILIO. El Muerte.

SANCHEZ. Not El Muerte. I could tell you his name but I won't. He'll taunt me and poke his finger at me and jab me with his scrawny hand, his bony fist. His dead eyes will see nothing and I will fight him. And because I have a stripe and a gong and my picture in the newspaper and contempt for their orgies and their gambling I would have no ally in the pack. They'd set on me like dogs and that's when they'd shit on me and slash me with their knives and leave me to spend the rest of the night dyin' in excrement. So. I've chosen to stay in. And celebrate. With you.

EMILIO *has stopped eating barely halfway through his first burger.*

EMILIO. Can't eat no more.

SANCHEZ. You said you were starvin'.

EMILIO. I was.

SANCHEZ. That cost me ten dollars.

EMILIO. Lost my appetite.

SANCHEZ. Whassamadder?

EMILIO. Nothin'.

SANCHEZ. 'fraida girls?

EMILIO. No.

SANCHEZ. You watch how I do it with the fat one.

SANCHEZ *takes the stetson from his head and puts it on* EMILIO's.

SANCHEZ. Eighty dollars that cost me. Thass a lotta money. More'n they cost in Texas. It's all yours.

EMILIO. Thanks.

SANCHEZ. Eat up.

EMILIO *takes a bite.*

SANCHEZ. El Muerte's my buddy now. I got him out of Ocotal.

EMILIO. How?

SANCHEZ. He's comin' with us.

EMILIO *chokes*.

SANCHEZ. On our special mission.

EMILIO. Who else?

SANCHEZ. You seen El Chino yet?

EMILIO. No.

SANCHEZ. You'd better have a session with El Chino before we go forth on our mission. Did Icaza mention me?

EMILIO. When?

SANCHEZ. Today. Did 'e mention my decoration? My medal?

EMILIO. Yes.

SANCHEZ. Good.

EMILIO *sits with the stetson on his head, the two beefburgers in his hands*.

SANCHEZ. What did he say?

EMILIO. Who?

SANCHEZ. Icaza.

EMILIO. Nothin' much.

SANCHEZ. I'd like to know what he said.

EMILIO. He said you were stupid.

SANCHEZ. What?

EMILIO. No. He said you must be stupid if . . .

SANCHEZ. Icaza said that?

EMILIO. Well . . .

SANCHEZ. Me? Stupid?

EMILIO. No, he . . .

SANCHEZ. What else did he say?

EMILIO. Nothin' much.

SANCHEZ. Did he say you were stupid?

EMILIO. No.

SANCHEZ. What did he say about you?

EMILIO. He thinks I'm very clever.

SANCHEZ. What else?

EMILIO. What?

SANCHEZ. Did you talk about?

EMILIO. Talked about the baseball.

SANCHEZ. Yesterday's match?

EMILIO. He told me I'm a very gifted sportsman.

SANCHEZ. He's never said that to me.

EMILIO *is silent.*

SANCHEZ. He's never said that to me.

EMILIO *is silent.*

SANCHEZ. About my baseball.

EMILIO. That's because he thinks you're a lousy player.

SANCHEZ. Is that what he said?

EMILIO. Yes.

SANCHEZ. Who's bastard welfare session was this?

EMILIO. You asked me what he said . . .

SANCHEZ. I got you out of Ocotal is that stupid?

EMILIO. Icaza said the way I pitched yesterday I'm more or less certain of a place on the team.

SANCHEZ. Which team?

EMILIO. Kirkpatrick Cowboys.

SANCHEZ. Kirkpatrick Cowboys! You gotta be Joe di Maggio to play with them!

EMILIO. He reckoned I pitched well enough to avoid the risk of bein' sent to Ocotal.

SANCHEZ. What the hell is that supposed to mean?

EMILIO. Means Icaza got me out of Ocotal.

SANCHEZ. I got you out of Ocotal!

EMILIO. Icaza said . . .

SANCHEZ. Icaza's nobody!

EMILIO. He said . . .

SANCHEZ. I don't give a shit!

EMILIO. He said . . .

SANCHEZ. Shuttup!

EMILIO. You asked . . .

SANCHEZ. I never asked!

EMILIO. You said . . .

SANCHEZ. I never said!

EMILIO. You said . . .

SANCHEZ. Shuttup!

EMILIO. . . . what did he say . . .

SANCHEZ. I don't wanna know!

EMILIO. I'm tellin' you what you said!

SANCHEZ. I know what I said!

EMILIO. I'm tellin' you what he said!

SANCHEZ. I know what he said!

EMILIO. You don't!

SANCHEZ. I do!

EMILIO. You don't know . . .

SANCHEZ. I do!

EMILIO. I never said . . .

SANCHEZ (*yells*). I know what I said!

SANCHEZ *drinks.*

EMILIO *places the beefburgers carefully on the floor beside the chair.*

SANCHEZ. What else did 'e say?

EMILIO. Nothin' much.

SANCHEZ. Icaza's a judge. He doesn't go round makin'
pronouncements like that about men who've had a medal
pinned on their chest. He's a leader. He understands men like
me. He knows what makes us tick and he builds on that, brick
upon brick an army. And I'm the hero. I'm a decorated man!

EMILIO. Yes.

SANCHEZ. In the eyes of some a God. My S-1 said that. He
said El Phudd you know in the Honduran sector they're callin'
you a God? I said I know that sir he said don't take it to heart
he said there's only one God I said I know that. He said don't
start believin' you're immortal just because some Honduran
said you're a God. He said watch your step. He said you're up
against cunning. Butchers. Coyotes. Dogs. Beggardogs. The
biters off of babies' heads. The inoculators of piss into the
arms of the innocent. The Sandinistas.

EMILIO *nods.*

SANCHEZ. Uh?

EMILIO. Yes.

SANCHEZ. So. Now. For fuck sake. Celebrate.

EMILIO *sips rum.*

SANCHEZ *finds his roll of bills and walks round the hut putting piles
of bills in strategic places – under chairs, under mattresses, on pillows,
inside one of* EMILIO*'s burgers etc . . .*

SANCHEZ. . . . getta coupla girls in, no better way just the two
of us and a coupla girls, few laughs, few giggles, get drunk, get
their clothes off, get 'em walkin' round, parading up and down
stark naked tits goin' this way and that, throw dollars at 'em,
that's what you do, throw dollars at 'em 'cos there's nothing'
they won't do for dollars and I got eight hundred of 'em so
we're in for one helluva night 'cos eight hundred dollars is
more'n they'd expect to see in a month the two of 'em so
there's nothing. Nothing those girls won't do for us tonight.

EMILIO *is glum at the prospect.*

SANCHEZ. Gonna smile?

EMILIO *smiles.*

SANCHEZ. There's only one thing I won't do for money that's
take a human life. Icaza knows that. 'Cos I've told him and he
respects that. There's got to be a reason for what I do. Killin'
for money is worse than killin' for fun. There's hundreds here
do both but killin' for money's worse than killin' for fun in my
book. You got to have a reason.

EMILIO. You killed my father for money.

SANCHEZ. He was a Communist. I destroy Communism. He was a Communist Official. An instrument of evil. That's my reason. That's why I killed 'im.

EMILIO. The Gringo paid you five hundred dollars.

SANCHEZ. He did not.

EMILIO. I saw him.

A knock at the door.

SANCHEZ. Ah.

SANCHEZ *rises and presses the button on the ghetto-blaster.*

'Ramrod' plays. He takes the stetson off EMILIO*'s head.*

SANCHEZ (*to* EMILIO). Dance.

SANCHEZ *prepares himself for the* GIRLS.

Another knock.

SANCHEZ. Wait!

He smooths his hair and places the stetson carefully back on his head. He adjusts his shirt etc, then heads for the door and looks back at EMILIO.

SANCHEZ. Dance. Fuck you can't you dance?

EMILIO. I'm gonna be sick.

EMILIO *covers his mouth.* SANCHEZ *leaps across and bends him double.*

SANCHEZ. Lift your lungs up!

Another knock.

Wait! Don't come in! Shit!

SANCHEZ *puts his hand over* EMILIO*'s mouth. He wedges his other hand under* EMILIO*'s diaphragm, hoists his stomach up and bends over at the same time.*

EMILIO *and* SANCHEZ *are bent double.*

The door opens cautiously. Enter the CONTRA.

SANCHEZ. Whaddaya want!

CONTRA. Ten dollars.

SANCHEZ. I say ten dollars?

CONTRA. Yes.

SANCHEZ. For fetchin' two burgers? Which he didn't eat?

CONTRA. That was the deal.

SANCHEZ. Well fuck you!

CONTRA. You're El Phudd ain't you?

SANCHEZ. Yeah. (*To* EMILIO.) Start dancin'. (*To* CONTRA). Seen two girls?

CONTRA. No.

SANCHEZ. What's your name?

CONTRA. Vulture.

SANCHEZ. You goin' to Ocotal?

VULTURE. Yup.

SANCHEZ (*confidentially*). Wanna get out of Ocotal?

CONTRA. How?

SANCHEZ. Leave it to El Phudd. Here's a twenty.

SANCHEZ *hands* VULTURE *a twenty dollar bill and shuts the door. He dances an obscene shuffle with the bottle clutched to his cheek.*

EMILIO *jigs in a corner.*

The door opens and a SKINNY GIRL *enters. She watches them dance.*

EMILIO *is the first to notice her. He stops dancing.* SANCHEZ *sees the girl and stops dancing.*

SANCHEZ. Where is she? Where's the fat one! Where's Maria!

The GIRL *holds her arms out to* SANCHEZ *and twitches her hips.*

SANCHEZ. Maria! I want Maria!

GIRL. She's in the bushes.

SANCHEZ. Uh?

GIRL. She went with Vulture. He gave her a twenny.

SANCHEZ *exits.*

SANCHEZ (*from off-stage*). Come back! Maria! Vulture! Fuck you! Come here!

He disappears into the night.

EMILIO *switches off the tape.*

GIRL. Wanna girlfriend?

EMILIO. No.

GIRL. You don't wanna girlfriend?

EMILIO. You want some money?

EMILIO gathers up some of the money SANCHEZ planted about the place. He hands the GIRL about one hundred dollars. The girl can't believe her luck.

GIRL. You don't wanna girlfriend?

EMILIO. No.

GIRL. It's your money jack.

EMILIO. Go home. Quick.

The sound of SANCHEZ puking outside.

GIRL. If that's the way you wannit.

The GIRL pockets the money and runs.

Enter SANCHEZ, wiping his mouth.

SANCHEZ. She gone?

EMILIO. Yeah.

SANCHEZ. Pay 'er?

EMILIO. Yes.

SANCHEZ. How much?

EMILIO. Hundred.

SANCHEZ. Hundred? . . . What for . . . you fuck her?

EMILIO. Yes.

SANCHEZ looks at his watch. He looks at EMILIO.

SANCHEZ. For a hundred bucks? You gave her a hundred?

EMILIO shrugs.

SANCHEZ. You shittin' on me?

EMILIO. What?

SANCHEZ. You orchestrate this? You and Vulture?

EMILIO. Who? No!

SANCHEZ. Kiss the Pope.

EMILIO *kisses the Pope.*

SANCHEZ. You got me to thank, for all this. I brought you here. This is freedom. This is democracy.

SANCHEZ *pinions* EMILIO *to the wall with his thumb and forefinger.*

SANCHEZ. There's one thing money can't buy in this place. Know what that is?

EMILIO. No.

SANCHEZ. Buddies. You're my buddy and I'm your buddy. We ain't got no other buddies 'cos buddies don't grow on trees. So when you find a buddy you stick with him.

EMILIO. Your breath stinks.

SANCHEZ. With me?

EMILIO. Yes.

SANCHEZ. You're not a Communist are you.

EMILIO. I'm not a Communist I swear.

SANCHEZ. You've sworn before his holiness.

EMILIO. Yes.

SANCHEZ *takes his rosary from his pocket.*

SANCHEZ (*to himself*). Fat cow. Fat bitch.

He lies on the mattress praying and counting his beads.

EMILIO *sits leaning against the Pope.*

EMILIO. I had a girlfriend once. In Managua. When I was shining shoes. Her father and mother had bin killed by the Contras so she and her two sisters came down to Managua. I met her the first day I was there. She was shining shoes and I shone shoes. She didn't make as much as me because men don't like women cleaning their shoes and there wasn't many women wore leather. My girlfriend never wore shoes. I shone shoes in the street, she shone shoes in the restaurants. She reckoned restaurants were the best. She'd go in there and offer a price for the whole table then slide under and get crackin'. For some reason men found it more acceptable to have a woman shine their shoes if she was under a table. Pesca Fresca. That's where she operated. I offered her my shoes once. Not to clean. To wear. They were too big. She took me

home. She had a home. The Sandinista defence Committee
saw to that. She made enough under the table to feed her two
sisters. She reckoned before the Revolution if she was on the
streets she woulda bin a prostitute but there wasn't many girls
her age on the game. She made enough to get by which was a
miracle because before the Triumph there wasn't one man
who woulda let her shine his shoes under the table or on it.
That's emancipation she said. She reckoned Women's
struggles had a long way to go before she could afford shoes
shinin' shoes. And by the time it had she woulda moved on to
something else. She could read.

SANCHEZ (*half asleep*). Was she fat?

EMILIO. Can't remember.

SANCHEZ *is asleep*.

EMILIO *faces the Pope, crosses himself and takes from his pocket*
PEDRO's *bible. He kneels before the Pope and reads the bible.*

Scene Four
CAPTURE

Nicaragua
Three weeks later. Noon. A clearing in thick forest at the foot of a mountain.

EMILIO *stands alone. He carries a rucksack, Uzi automatic, water
canteen, sidearm, knife, poncho liner, tent etc.*

Howler monkeys squeal. Bullfrogs croak. Cicadas rattle.

SANCHEZ *enters. He looks round him and unbuckles his backpack.*

EMILIO. We stopping here?

SANCHEZ *drinks water.*

EMILIO. We're at the foot of a mountain.

SANCHEZ *takes a bottle of pills from his rucksack and swallows a
handful with water.*

EMILIO. What about the rendezvous? (*Checks his watch.*) We
arranged to meet El Muerte at the top of the mountain. El
Muerte said . . .

SANCHEZ. I'm commander of this patrol. Not you. Not El
Muerte. Not Vulture. Me.

EMILIO. We lost?

SANCHEZ. No.

SANCHEZ *unfolds a map and lays it on the ground.*

EMILIO. Where are we?

SANCHEZ. Not sure.

EMILIO *takes a campagaz from his rucksack.*

EMILIO. What about El Muerte and Vulture?

SANCHEZ. Put that back.

EMILIO *does as he's told.*

SANCHEZ. Keep your boots on. Don't even take 'em off to air your feet. It's dense round this clearing. Perfect ambush country. Remember. If we're attacked. Run into it. They expect you to retreat and plant all their firepower behind you. They're weakest up front so run into the attack. Spray 'em. These Uzi's are better than their AK's. These talk. These spit fire.

SANCHEZ *takes the Pope from his pocket. He kisses it and passes it to* EMILIO.

EMILIO *kisses the Pope and pockets it.*

EMILIO. Wish El Muerte was here.

SANCHEZ. El Muerte's nothing.

EMILIO. If he was here we wouldn't be lost.

SANCHEZ. We'd still be here.

EMILIO. That may be so. But we wouldn't be lost.

SANCHEZ. We're not lost.

EMILIO. We don't know where we are.

SANCHEZ. We do.

EMILIO. We don't.

SANCHEZ. It's thanks to you we are lost.

EMILIO. So we are lost.

SANCHEZ. We're not . . .

EMILIO. You said . . .

SANCHEZ. I said nothin' . . .

EMILIO. You . . .

SANCHEZ. You know what El Muerte said? To me? He said c'mon leave the little shit behind he's so slow 'e said . . .

EMILIO. I heard what he said.

SANCHEZ. He said leave him stew. He's holding us back.

EMILIO. I heard.

SANCHEZ. I said no. You go on I said. I'll stay with him. Hear that?

EMILIO. No.

SANCHEZ. I could be with El Muerte now but I'm not I'm with you.

EMILIO. We're still lost.

SANCHEZ. Who survived Chachagua? Uh? The only one left alive. Outa Chachagua. Uh?

EMILIO. You were down the hill.

SANCHEZ. Exactly.

EMILIO. That's luck.

SANCHEZ. Luck?!

EMILIO. It's nothing to do with courage –

SANCHEZ. Luck?

EMILIO. Or training –

SANCHEZ. Yes it is –

EMILIO. Or initiative. Or skill. Or strength. Or guile.

SANCHEZ. It's all those things.

EMILIO. El Muerte don't rely on luck.

SANCHEZ. It was no fuckin' luck bein' saddled with you!

EMILIO. El Muerte can read a map.

SANCHEZ. To be let loose with you in the middle of nowhere's no fuckin' luck!

EMILIO. El Muerte said all that El Phudd the hero guff's beating the drum for Ocotal –

SANCHEZ. No 'e didn't.

EMILIO. He said they print all that in the newspapers before a big offensive to boost moral –

SANCHEZ. That's lies.

EMILIO. He said they make damn sure they don't take El Phudd
   to Ocotal or the men will see he's a bigger coward than they are –

SANCHEZ. You're tellin' lies!

EMILIO. I'd sooner be at Ocotal than here.

SANCHEZ. That shows how fuckin' ignorant you are.

EMILIO. I am ignorant.

SANCHEZ. Gimme the Pope.

EMILIO. And slow.

SANCHEZ. Pope.

EMILIO. And scared.

SANCHEZ. Where's the Pope.

EMILIO. I can't fight.

SANCHEZ. Where is 'e?

EMILIO. Why choose me?

SANCHEZ. Where's the Pope?

EMILIO. Pope's no good.

SANCHEZ. Hand it over.

EMILIO. Pope ain't gonna read a map . . .

SANCHEZ. Gimme the Pope!

EMILIO. Pope ain't gonna protect us –

SANCHEZ. Come on!

   EMILIO *has the Pope in his hand.*

EMILIO. Pope ain't gonna part the jungle and swallow up the
   beggardogs –

SANCHEZ. Give it here.

EMILIO. Pope ain't gonna stop 'em injecting us with piss –

SANCHEZ. Shuttup!

EMILIO. Pope ain't gonna tie our balls back on!

   EMILIO *tears the Pope to shreds.*

EMILIO. There! Kiss that!

SANCHEZ. You imbecile! You don't understand! I'll kill you
for this!

EMILIO. You never killed anyone who wasn't stripped naked
and tied to a tree!

SANCHEZ *unsheaths his knife.*

EMILIO *dances out of the way. He taunts* SANCHEZ.

EMILIO. You ain't got the guts to kill me. You're too stupid.
You're a coward. You're a fraud. You're a fool. You're
nothing on your own. Nothing. Without me. Nothing.
Without the Pope.

SANCHEZ *points at the remains of the Pope scattered across the clearing.*

SANCHEZ. Pick 'em up.

EMILIO. No.

SANCHEZ. Pick 'em up.

EMILIO. No.

SANCHEZ *stalks* EMILIO.

SANCHEZ. This is a damned serious business. Disobeying the
orders of your patrol commander. Pick up the Pope.

EMILIO. No.

SANCHEZ. It's mutiny. And the price of mutiny is death. In any
army in every war that's ever been in the whole history of the
world from Adam on the penalty is death. So. Pick the Pope up.

EMILIO. No.

SANCHEZ *launches himself at* EMILIO *and grabs him. He places
the blade of his knife at* EMILIO*'s throat.*

SANCHEZ. You've made a big mistake. I'm no fool 'cos I'm
alive. Y'understand? If I was a fool I'd be dead. But I'm alive.
And I'm stayin' alive. You started to get the wrong ideas
about what's right and what's wrong and who's lost and who's
found and it's begun to wear me out. There's no such thing as
lost and found it's alive or dead. You think El Muerte's still
alive I bet you a thousand dollars he's dead and you're gonna
join 'im!

A chorus of clicks all round the clearing, off-stage.

SANCHEZ *freezes.*

Enter six SANDINISTA SOLDIERS.

They are aged 15 to 17. A fast, efficient entrance.

MIGUEL *and* EDWIN *patrol the perimeter of the clearing.*

JUANITA *and* PABLO *disarm and frisk* EMILIO *and* SANCHEZ.

HERNANDEZ *speaks to* RICO, *the wireless operator.*

HERNANDEZ. Radio Phantom. Tell 'em we got two Contra prisoners aged (*To* EMILIO.) how old are you kid?

EMILIO. Fifteen.

HERNANDEZ (*to* RICO). Fifteen and (*To* SANCHEZ.) what's your age son?

SANCHEZ *points at* EMILIO.

SANCHEZ. He killed my father. I watched him do it.

HERNANDEZ (*guessing*). Seventeen.

RICO *starts to tinker with the radio.* PABLO *trawls through their rucksacks.*

SANCHEZ. He's crazy. He skinned my father alive. I saw him. Yanked his skin off like a coat.

HERNANDEZ. – We want 'em picked up.

JUANITA. We stopping here?

HERNANDEZ. Give him five minutes on the radio.

PABLO *finds a can of beans and opens them.*

EMILIO. That's not true.

JUANITA. What?

EMILIO. He killed *my* father.

SANCHEZ. See? He's crazy.

EMILIO. He's twisting it.

SANCHEZ. Don't listen to him.

PABLO *eats beans.*

EMILIO. I never killed anyone.

SANCHEZ. Watch out for this kid. He's unstable. He has a mental history.

EMILIO. He's lying.

SANCHEZ. I've seen him strip a man naked, tie him to a tree and mutilate him for no reason.

EMILIO. That's what he did to my father.

SANCHEZ. What kind of mind is that uh? Fifteen years old. Beyond redemption.

EMILIO. Liar!

PABLO *offers the beans to* MIGUEL.

SANCHEZ. I want justice. I want him strung up.

JUANITA. You'll get justice.

SANCHEZ. I want him shot. Now.

EMILIO. I didn't touch his father!

SANCHEZ. I tell you he's not worth keeping. He's crazy.

EMILIO. He killed my father! I watched him do it! He hacked him to pieces he did it for the money!

SANCHEZ. I did not!

EMILIO. See?

SANCHEZ. I did not kill him!

EMILIO. For five hundred bucks!

SANCHEZ. No!

RICO. For chrissake!

EMILIO. I want justice.

PABLO *takes the beans from* MIGUEL *and offers them to* HERNANDEZ.

PABLO. Beans?

EMILIO. I want him punished!

JUANITA. He will be if he did it.

EMILIO. I want him dead!

SANCHEZ. Listen to that.

EMILIO. I tried to forgive him.

JUANITA. Takes years.

EMILIO. I read the Bible, read the gospels –

SANCHEZ. There's nothing to forgive –

EMILIO. I searched the Bible for guidance –

SANCHEZ. There's nothing to forgive –

EMILIO. I stared at the Pope on the wall of the hut for days, searched his face –

SANCHEZ. You treacherous bastard! I saved your life! You shit on me? I'm your buddy. Y'know what they do, back in Honduras to men who betray their buddies? Know what they do? To men who shit on their friends? I've seen 'em. And that's what you're gonna get.

EMILIO. We're not goin' back to Honduras.

SANCHEZ. Yes we are.

EMILIO. You're losing your mind.

SANCHEZ. I'm not!

EMILIO. We're captured. We're prisoners.

SANCHEZ. You wait. You wait.

EMILIO. I never betrayed anybody.

SANCHEZ. Dog.

EMILIO. I'm notta dog.

SANCHEZ. Murderer.

EMILIO (*screams*). I didn't touch his father! He's lying! He killed *my* father. I never killed anyone! I swear I'm telling the truth! You've got to believe me! I never killed anyone! I never killed anyone!

The nightmare is too much for him. He falls to the ground where he remains immobile, speechless, but conscious.

RICO. This radio's fucked.

HERNANDEZ. Get through?

RICO. No.

HERNANDEZ. Shit.

HERNANDEZ, PABLO *and* JUANITA *crouch round the radio.* HERNANDEZ *fiddles with the radio.* MIGUEL *and* EDWIN *guard the prisoners.*

EDWIN *speaks to* SANCHEZ.

EDWIN. Don't worry. If he murdered your father the truth will out.

SANCHEZ. How?

EDWIN *considers.*

SANCHEZ. See? How?

EDWIN. Witnesses?

SANCHEZ. They're all dead.

EDWIN. I know what I'm talking about, believe me. We'll take him back to Matagalpa, he'll go in a prison, open prison for Contras, he'll learn a trade, raise a pig, few roosters, he gets rehabilitated. He begins to understand that nobody's gonna cut his balls off, nobody's gonna kill him. He's back amongst his own people. Soon he's no longer a Contra. He's a different person. And then he says back when I was a Contra I killed this guy's father, because I was a Contra. But I'm not a Contra anymore. See? So. He's confessed! Then you come along and say look, nobody can bring my father back, I still can't forgive you. But I can at least understand why you did it. Because you were a Contra. Incidentally you're not a Contra any more either. And he says I don't want your forgiveness yet, but in ten, twenty years let's meet again. OK? So you say yup. You shake hands and part company. See? That's how it works. The same thing happened to my brother.

SANCHEZ *considers this. At length he speaks.*

SANCHEZ. Gotta Pope?

EDWIN. Uh?

SANCHEZ. Anybody gotta Pope?

MIGUEL *and* EDWIN *both offer Popes.*

SANCHEZ *takes* EDWIN'*s. He kisses the Pope and stares at the picture.*

EDWIN. I had six Popes once. Pious, John, Peter and three John Pauls. I exchanged Pious for a pair of shoes. I thought it was blasphemous at the time but I know better now. I buried John with my brother. I lost Peter and two John Pauls went up in smoke with my house.

HERNANDEZ *stands. He kicks the radio.*

HERNANDEZ. Junk.

PABLO. Now what?

HERNANDEZ. We can't leave the sector unpatrolled.

JUANITA (*indicates prisoners*). What are we gonna do with them?

HERNANDEZ. Take 'em with us.

PABLO. On patrol?

JUANITA. What else?

They study the prisoners.

JUANITA *examines* EMILIO.

JUANITA. He's catatonic.

EDWIN. My brother had that.

HERNANDEZ. We'll have to carry him.

PABLO. This is crazy.

HERNANDEZ. We'll head east to Muy-muy, and wait there for Fonseca patrol, that do you?

PABLO. Why can't we go south to Esteli?

HERNANDEZ. Because we can't leave the sector.

PABLO *shrugs.*

HERNANDEZ. Best we can do without a radio.

They prepare to leave.

HERNANDEZ *indicates the prisoners.*

HERNANDEZ. Tie 'em up.

MIGUEL *ties their hands in front of them.*

SANCHEZ *still holds the Pope.*

EMILIO *remains on the ground.*

EDWIN *has been inspecting the radio. He rises and wanders over to the prisoners.*

EDWIN. My brother was a magician with radios. He made one
  outa wood when he was ten.

MIGUEL. Outa wood?

EDWIN. I first heard Michael Jackson on that radio.

MIGUEL. You can't make a radio outa wood.

EDWIN. My brother did.

MIGUEL. That's impossible.

EDWIN. He did it.

MIGUEL. He woulda stolen the radio from a car and put it in a
  wooden box to hide it from the Guardia.

EDWIN. No.

MIGUEL. You ever see inside this radio?

EDWIN. Yes.

MIGUEL. What were the insides made of?

EDWIN. Wood.

MIGUEL. And you heard Michael Jackson on this?

EDWIN. Yes.

MIGUEL. What did 'e sound like?

EDWIN. Very faint.

  MIGUEL *has stopped tying the prisoners' hands together.*

  SANCHEZ *holds out the Pope to him.*

SANCHEZ. Read the back.

  MIGUEL *reads the back.*

MIGUEL. Between God and the Revolution there is no
conflict.

  He hands the Pope back to SANCHEZ. *They are ready to leave.*

  PABLO *picks* EMILIO *up and stands him straight. He steadies*
  EMILIO *while* HERNANDEZ *hoists him over his shoulder.*

  SANCHEZ *kisses the Pope and drops him to the ground. They exit*
  individually.

JUANITA *goes first, she is followed at five second intervals by:*
HERNANDEZ/EMILIO, EDWIN, SANCHEZ, MIGUEL,
RICO, PABLO.

Monkeys howl.

The Pope remains, centre stage.

END